A Church for the Future

**South Africa as the Crucible for Anglicanism
in a New Century**

Harold T. Lewis

CHURCH PUBLISHING
an imprint of
Church Publishing Incorporated, New York

Church Publishing Incorporated
445 Fifth Avenue
New York NY 10016
www.churchpublishing.org

Cover design by Brycen Davis
Interior design by Linda Brooks

Library of Congress Cataloging-in-Publication Data

Lewis, Harold T.
A Church for the future: South Africa and the future of Anglicanism / Harold T. Lewis.
    p. cm.
Includes bibliographical references (p. 155).
ISBN 978-0-89869-566-3 (pbk.)
1. Church of England—South Africa—History—21st century. 2. Anglican Communion—South Africa—History—21st century. 3. South Africa—Church history. I. Title.

 BX5700.6.A4L49 2007
 283'.6809051--dc22

 2007026195

Printed in the United States of America

5 4 3 2 1

To my students at
The College of the Transfiguration, Grahamstown,
from whom I learned a great deal
about the History, Mission and Ethos of
The Church in South Africa

TABLE OF CONTENTS

vii

ACKNOWLEDGMENTS

I wish to express my thanks to the wardens and vestry of Calvary Church, Pittsburgh, Pennsylvania, for a sabbatical leave in 2004 which I spent in South Africa as a visiting lecturer at the College of Transfiguration in Grahamstown. I am also grateful to the Lilly Endowment, Inc., for a generous Clergy Renewal Grant, which underwrote travel and living expenses.

Canon Livingston Ngewu, Rector of the College, was a solicitous host. Our conversations about everything from church history to the Mother's Union and our memorable and enlightening trip to Umtata and Kokstad gave me a deeper understanding of the South African church than I would otherwise have had. The faculty, staff and students at "COT" were warm and cordial to me and my wife, Claudette, for the duration of our stay. Our time there was truly a period of refreshment on many levels. The daily round of worship in the seminary chapel (where I became proficient at the marimba); breaking bread in the refectory with the community; and chatting informally with students in the common room enriched the time I spent in the classroom, where I learned far more than I taught. And how can we forget the weekend *braais* (South African barbecues) at Kenton-on-Sea?

Archbishops Desmond Tutu and Njongonkulu Ndungane, Bishops Michael Nuttall and Thabo Makgoba, Professor Jonathan Draper and Canon Luke Pato were kind enough to grant me interviews, which proved invaluable to my research. I am also deeply grateful to Dr. Mongezi Guma, rector of the Church of Christ the King, Sophiatown, for inviting me to attend the inaugural *Naught for Your Comfort* lecture there, in honor of Trevor Huddleston, CR. I am also appreciative for having been accorded the privilege of preaching in that parish's historic pulpit, although I wish I had been warned that Archbishop Tutu would be in the congregation! I am indebted to Nancy and Milton Washington, who again created a writing studio for me at their lovely home on Martha's Vineyard.

My hat goes off to my two editors. Jonathan Reiber's knowledge and love of South Africa as well as his scholarship assisted me immeasurably in determining the shape and focus of this book. Frank Tedeschi's advice and counsel, born of his commitment to the mission of the church and his consummate skills as editor, served to make the rough places plain on the road to publication. Finally, I am grateful to Ken Arnold, former vice-president of Church Publishing, and the Reverend Tom Blackmon, Church Pension Fund's liaison to Church Publishing, for their guidance and support.

Harold T. Lewis
Pittsburgh
The Feast of Perpetua and her Companions, Martyrs at Carthage, 2007

FOREWORD

We are all in enormous debt to Harold Lewis for this book in which he situates Anglicanism in the profound position to lead the church catholic. Of course, this is no enviable task in light of the challenges that the Anglican Church currently faces; but the reader will find here significant history, together with provocative challenges and thoughts about the future of the Anglican Communion. I cite two reasons here for why I think this to be the case.

First, Lewis provides us all an important perspective on the future in light of the Anglican Church's past. This connection is particularly noteworthy when connected to the fledgling South African Church about which the first Lambeth Conference was convened. From little-known facts like this to profound analysis, Lewis leads the reader to new discoveries and insights that enable truth telling and reconciliation. Without such practices there will be no future.

Secondly, it is important to know about the Anglican Church in South Africa because we, in many ways, represent the faith of St. Paul—that is, we must never give up, even on a most contentious church community like Corinth. He writes, "We are hard pressed on every side, but not crushed; perplexed, but not in despair" (2 Corinthians 4:8). Paul's eloquence encourages us first to see that there is a future for our church, and second, to know that this future is only accomplished through God's ultimate work of transfiguration. Such work is not only our hope but our faith.

In conclusion, Harold Lewis invites us ultimately into a beatific vision seldom seen. Unlike our past western church history, many eyes are now on the African church. It is my prayer that we will all learn from the mistakes of the past—that is, wandering in the wilderness of violence and oppression—so that we can flourish now and in the future. This is calling of us all to the promised land of God's reign on earth.

✠ Desmond Mpilo Tutu
Cape Town, South Africa
The Feast of the Transfiguration, 2007

INTRODUCTION

The Anomaly of the South African Church

Grahamstown was the first English settlement in South Africa. It is not surprising, therefore, that when the Anglican Church began to expand beyond the environs of Cape Town, Grahamstown was chosen as the see city of South Africa's second diocese. At the east end of that city's High Street sits the Cathedral Church of St. Michael and St. George. Its steeple dominates the skyline. East of the Cathedral are Grahamstown's townships, or "locations," home to the overwhelming majority of its black population. At the west end of High Street is the entrance to the campus of Rhodes University, established by a bequest from the estate of Cecil Rhodes, the Victorian industrialist and empire-builder. Adjacent to that campus is the College of the Transfiguration, the official seminary of the Church in the Province of Southern Africa. That institution began its life a hundred years ago as St. Paul's Theological College, whose mission it was to prepare South Africa's white sons for the ordained ministry. Today, women and men, black, white and colored, from South Africa, Namibia, Angola, Lesotho, Mozambique and Swaziland (the nations whose dioceses are in the province) as well as other African nations, make up the student body.

I arrived at COT (the seminary's acronym and nickname) in January of 2004, to spend my sabbatical leave there as a visiting lecturer. I found that two recent developments in the Anglican world dominated the conversations in the common room. One was the consecration two months earlier of Canon V. Gene

Robinson as bishop of New Hampshire. Normally, such an event, occurring in a diocese of some forty parishes in one of the smallest states in the American Republic would not be newsworthy in a town in the Eastern Cape of South Africa. But the elevation to the episcopacy of Robinson, an openly gay and partnered priest, had become front-page news in even the remotest hamlets of the Anglican Communion. The second news item was that the next Lambeth Conference, the decennial gathering of the world's Anglican bishops, was to take place in Cape Town in 2008, marking the first time since 1867 that that event would not take place in England. There was a palpable pride on the faces of the seminary community, in the knowledge that the South African church had been so recognized. It represented, in many ways, a coming of age of the African Church, and a realization that the strength of Anglicanism was no longer in the British Isles, but in the Global South.

An interesting thread connected these two events in the personage of Njongonkulu Winston Hugh Ndungane, the archbishop of Cape Town. Ndungane, as primate, had issued the invitation to come to South Africa to his brother and sister bishops, an invitation which met with the enthusiasm of the Archbishop of Canterbury and the Anglican Consultative Council. It was also Ndungane who had distinguished himself by speaking out in favor of Robinson's consecration at a time when his fellow African primates had denounced it as unbiblical and immoral, and as a grave threat to the unity of the Anglican Communion. In many instances, primates even declared that their churches were, on account of this development, in impaired communion with the Episcopal Church USA. I was intrigued that the Church in the Province of Southern Africa was the sole dissenting voice on this issue among the twelve provinces on the African continent, and this book was begun as an effort to probe into the reasons for that anomaly.

The first thing I discovered was a fascinating piece of history which threw some light on the current situation. The first Lambeth Conference, convened in 1867 by Charles Thomas Longley, Archbishop of Canterbury from 1862 to 1868, came into being because of an internal problem within the fledgling South African church. In 1863, Robert Gray, Bishop of Cape Town, deposed John William Colenso from the ordained ministry. Alleging that his writings did "contravene and subvert the Catholic Faith," Gray declared Colenso a heretic and removed him from office. Though excommunicated, Colenso appealed to the English courts, and, owing largely to a legal technicality, was reinstated.

This resulted in an untenable situation in which two bishops, Colenso and the cleric whom Gray appointed to succeed him, claimed jurisdiction in the same diocese. Although this was an internal issue, bishops elsewhere in the Anglican Church convinced Archbishop Longley that it had grave implications for the entire Communion, and the first Lambeth Conference was convened to sort things out. That process was significant. It laid the groundwork for the structure of the Anglican Communion, which with some modifications has endured until today. Second, it became clear that in the eyes of many, Colenso's crime was not heresy so much as it was a radical approach to mission. That approach set the stage for missionary endeavor which also has had a lasting effect on the life and witness of the church.

In subsequent chapters, I examine the effect of two other historical developments in the life of the South African church, in an attempt to understand what effect they might have on the social and theological stance of the province which distinguishes it from her sister churches in Africa. The first of these is the effect of Anglo-Catholicism on the social witness of the South African church. Most of the colonies in East Africa, notably Nigeria, Uganda and Kenya, were brought the Gospel by the evangelical Church Missionary Society. South Africa, on the other hand, was missionized by the Society for the Propagation of the Gospel, whose founders had been influenced by the catholic revival of the Oxford Movement. Knowing that so many bishops, clergy and religious in South Africa were Anglo-Catholics, a group known for their ministry among the poor and oppressed, I wanted to ask if the church's mission and theology bore the marks of an Anglo-Catholic ethos.

The other development I trace is the church's involvement in the struggle for racial justice in South Africa, and particularly its involvement in the anti-apartheid movement in the second half of the twentieth century. The implicit question asked here is whether striking a blow for justice on behalf of people of color might have had an effect on the way the church understands discrimination against other groups, notably women and gays, and justice issues as well.

Although we discuss the ministries of all of primates of the South African church, we make special mention of the two most recent incumbents. Desmond Mpilo Tutu, in his various leadership positions—Bishop of Lesotho, Dean of Johannesburg, Secretary General of the South African Council of Churches, Bishop of Johannesburg and Archbishop of Cape Town, did more than any other South African to bring about the eventual collapse of apartheid. Although clearly a "political animal," Tutu accomplished this not as an activist but as a theologian, declaring apartheid to be sin, because it denies the dignity of each human being. History might show, however, that his role as chair of the Truth and Reconciliation Commission, which brought so much healing to a divided nation, might be his greater legacy. Njongonkulu Ndungane, the present archbishop, has built upon Tutu's foundation, and has made it clear that poverty and AIDS are "new apartheids" which must be dismantled with even more dispatch than the original apartheid, in order that there will be a critical mass of South Africans able to enjoy the benefits of their newfound freedom.

The teachings of both men, as well as other South Africans, on the matter of human sexuality are highlighted toward the end of the book. I have called human sexuality an "iconic" issue rather than a "burning" issue, because I believe it has become emblematic of deeper issues that affect the Anglican family.

Finally, I argue that it is because of its unique social, ecclesiastical and theological history that South Africa will continue to be a crucible for the whole Communion. In the words of a South African bishop, it has "a pivotal and prophetic role to play in the healing of the present divisions in our communion, and particularly in our African context."

Chapter 1

Whither Lambeth? Anglicanism at the Crossroads

I request your presence at a meeting of the bishops in visible communion with the United Church of England and Ireland . . . I propose that, at our assembling, we should first solemnly seek the blessing of Almighty God on our gathering, by uniting together in the highest act of the Church's worship. After this brotherly consultations will follow. . . . Such a meeting would not be competent to make declarations or lay down definitions on points of doctrine. But united worship and common counsels would greatly tend to maintain practically the unity of the faith; whilst they would bind us in straiter [sic] bonds of peace and brotherly charity.

—Charles Thomas Longley, Archbishop of Canterbury,
from his letter inviting bishops to the first Lambeth Conference

"Brotherly Counsel and Encouragement"

The Lambeth Conference, a gathering of all the bishops of the Anglican Communion convened by the Archbishop of Canterbury, has met, except for those times impeded by World Wars, roughly every ten years since the middle of the nineteenth century. Named for Lambeth Palace, the Archbishop's London residence where the meetings were originally held, it has for some time outgrown that venue, and in recent decades has taken place at the University of Kent, outside of Canterbury. A collegial and non-legislative body, the Conference has afforded bishops in attendance the opportunity to discuss and pass resolutions on matters affecting the life of the Anglican Communion. It has also spoken on certain all-encompassing issues which affect the entire global community, and when it does, the Lambeth Conference is generally assumed to speak for the whole Anglican Communion, although it is, in fact, one of its four official advisory bodies, called "instruments of unity." The other three are the Anglican Consultative Council, whose membership is comprised of representatives, in most cases a bishop, a priest and a layperson from each province; the Primates, made up of the heads (an archbishop or presiding bishop) of each province; and the Archbishop of Canterbury himself.

Historically, issues of theology, polity and liturgy have dominated the agenda. Because the Communion is made up of a number of autonomous churches, or provinces, in communion with the Archbishop of Canterbury,[1] it has long been considered advisable for the church's mitered leaders to meet in council and, in principle, to affirm unity in their diversity. But more and more, the bishops of the Lambeth Conference, not content simply to promulgate abstract theological statements, have deemed it appropriate to exercise their pastoral office. With each successive conference, they have voiced their opinions on social issues, thus providing guidance for Anglicanism's faithful as to how they might carry out their apostolate in the world in which they move, breathe, live and have their being.

In other words, the bishops have attempted to provide a moral compass for Anglicans dispersed around the globe. As the Primate of Canada stated at the opening of the 1968 Conference, "At its best, Lambeth sends forth a fresh, spontaneous response to the problems facing the Church and the world. Its words are not the Church's final decrees, but messages from the pilgrim Church sent out as she journeys."[2] In 1948, for example, Lambeth addressed the issue of racism, stating that "discrimination between men on the grounds of race alone is inconsistent with the principles of Christian religion." Ten years later, the Conference promulgated an historic (and controversial) document endorsing the responsible use of birth control. The tenth Lambeth Conference, which took place in the year of the assassinations of both Martin Luther King, Jr. and Robert Kennedy, decried the fact that resorting to violence and bloodshed had become commonplace. Stating that "the Kingdom of God is often advanced by revolutionary change following on a change of heart," the Conference resolved that the Christian Church "must be ready to support individual Christians as they search for justice even by means which sometimes seem extreme, for example, civil disobedience."[3]

Increasingly, the Conference has weighed in on global matters, and in its resolutions has both shared with the world its positions on them and has encouraged appropriate groups to take the necessary action to redress the issues in question. It is especially germane to our discussion to point out that the Lambeth bishops, at their 1988 meeting, declared that "the system of apartheid in South Africa is evil and especially repugnant because of the cruel way a tyrannical racist system is being upheld in the name of the Christian faith," and called upon the churches to bring pressure to bear on the South African regime to promote a genuine process of change toward a democratic political structure.[4]

At its most recent gathering, in 1998, the Lambeth Conference decried the fact that the two-thirds world is mired in debt. The assembled bishops called upon both the industrialized nations and the international banking community to consider ways to alleviate or even forgive that debt. Indeed, the Archbishop of Cape Town was one of the staunchest advocates of such a strategy. "We live in a world," he stated, "in which money has more powerful rights than human rights, a world governed and dominated by Mammon. Only amongst our faith communities does there seem to be any will to challenge Mammon."[5]

A Missed Opportunity

In 2008, for the first time in its history, the Lambeth Conference was scheduled to meet outside of England, indeed some six thousand miles to the south of London. At the invitation of Archbishop Njongonkulu Ndungane, Primate of the Church of the Province of Southern Africa,[6] the Lambeth Conference was to take place in Cape Town. Plans for the Conference, which was to be held in conjunction with an Anglican Gathering to which priests and laypeople were also to have been invited, were moving apace, but on 28 June 2004, Sue Parks, the 2008 Lambeth Conference administrator, along with Lambeth Conference design group members Bishop James Tengatenga of Southern Malawi and Fung Yi Wong of Hong Kong, announced that a shortage of funding led to the cancellation of the joint event and to a change in venue for the Conference itself. "Certain uncertainties contributed to the lack of confidence to raise the funds for 2008," Ms. Wong said. Ndungane, in expressing his disappointment, stated that since funding at the level of ten million dollars could not be guaranteed, "it would be impossible for us to host such a big undertaking."[7]

The design group for the Lambeth Conference were cognizant of the fact that Cape Town would be a far more expensive venue than the campus of the University of Kent, and for this reason, had sought extraordinary funding, reportedly from foundations and individuals, which did not materialize to the extent necessary. It should be pointed out, however, that well before fiscal problems manifested themselves, the Cape Town Lambeth Conference was threatened for other reasons. An article in the London *Sunday Times,* in fact, suggested that the change of venue was "the first big casualty of the church's schism over homosexuality." The newspaper attributed this to the concern among many Africans that the Conference should not be held in Africa, where the opposition to the ordination of a gay bishop was the strongest. Also, Africans were reportedly unhappy that the extraordinary costs of a Cape Town conference would be borne by Americans.[8] Moreover, Archbishop Peter Akinola of Nigeria, who had called the consecration of a gay bishop in the American Church a "Satanic attack" on the church, indicated that he might lead a boycott of the Lambeth Conference and that he would be joined by other African primates and many of the bishops in their respective provinces if it took place in South Africa, because South Africa's archbishop had repeatedly defended the Episcopal Church's actions on the grounds of its provincial autonomy.

In a church generally regarded as bound by tradition, the significance of this potential departure from tradition cannot be overstated. Cape Town, the oldest Anglican see on the continent of Africa, came into being in 1848 when Robert Gray was dispatched from England under the auspices of the Society for the Propagation of the Gospel (SPG).[9] (In a typical colonial decision, the Anglican community in Southern Africa had previously been under the jurisdiction of the bishop of Calcutta!) But the world's bishops had not planned to descend on Cape Town to commemorate the 160th anniversary of the official planting of Anglicanism in Africa. Nor would they have come, like the World Cup in 2010, to celebrate the coming of democracy to South Africa and the dismantling of apartheid. Rather, they were to convene in Cape Town primarily to recognize what may be called the coming of age of African

Anglicanism, as evidenced by the demographic shift of the Communion to the Global South. As Archbishop of Canterbury Rowan Williams commented, "New times require a new kind of Lambeth Conference."[10]

Were it to take place in South Africa, the fourteenth Lambeth Conference would bear testimony to the reality that of the world's eighty million Anglicans, some forty million of them are members of churches in the twelve provinces in Africa,[11] of whom more than ten million are said to be in Nigeria alone. These numbers exceed those of the traditional "sending churches" which have been long established strongholds of Anglicanism. There are 800,000 members of the Anglican Church of Canada and 2,300,000 in the Episcopal Church, USA. And although there are officially some twenty-six million Anglicans in Europe, mostly in the United Kingdom, it is largely assumed that these numbers are inflated because of the method of identifying who Anglicans are.[12] By any reckoning, however, most Anglicans live in Africa, and most of the world's Anglican bishops are also Africans. Indeed the 1998 Lambeth Conference was the first at which the bishops representing the sending churches "were outnumbered by the bishops from the Anglican churches of Africa, Asia and Oceania."[13]

This dramatic shift in Anglican demographics was an important factor in Archbishop Ndungane's suggestion that the Conference take place in his province. (As Provincial Executive Officer of the province, Ndungane, for similar reasons, had urged the Anglican Consultative Council to meet in South Africa. The ACC accepted his invitation, and he hosted them in Cape Town in 1993.) In his recent book, *A World with a Human Face,* he raises the question as to whether the Archbishop of Canterbury, as *primus inter pares* ("first among equals") should be the only primate who can convene the Lambeth Conference. He observes, too, that despite

> the recognition that the balance of membership of our Communion has . . . shifted hugely to the southern hemisphere, the vestiges of neo-colonialism and paternalism nonetheless remain enshrined in our Anglican institutions, and in our instruments of dialogue and unity. In this sense I would want us all to take a long look at the Lambeth Conference itself. . . . Is it morally defensible, for instance, in a diverse, global context that representatives of our family should return to the perceived 'motherland' for the conference?[14]

The fact that Lambeth XIV was to have been in Cape Town is recognition of a virtual sea change in Anglicanism. The exponential growth of the church in the two-thirds world is, arguably, an unforeseen consequence of British colonial expansion. As the Cross followed the Union Jack to the uttermost parts of the Empire on which the sun was said never to set, English missionaries brought the faith as the Anglican Church has received it to those whom Queen Victoria had made British subjects. The SPG, and its sister missionary organization, the more evangelical, "low church" Church Missionary Society (CMS),[15] perceived that they had a mandate, therefore, to "fling out the banner" and to bring the Gospel, to use the words of Bishop Heber's missionary hymn, to "Africa's sunny fountains."[16]

It is truly lamentable that in the opening decade of this new millennium the world's Anglican bishops will not meet in that corner of the globe where the Indian and Atlantic Oceans converge, for in so doing, they would have sent a message (regardless of whatever resolutions they would have passed at their gathering) that Anglicanism has irrevocably changed. For the shift in Anglican demographics does not simply mean that Anglicans are more broadly dispersed than before, or that there is now a heavier concentration of Anglicans in the southern hemisphere. It signals, among other things, that there are more Anglicans in the developing world than in the developed world, more poor Anglicans than rich, more black and brown Anglicans than white, more Anglicans who speak languages other than English than native English speakers. The shift means that the idea of Anglicans as "the Tory party at prayer" must be scrapped. It means that an Anglicanism thought to be the spiritual refuge of the privileged classes is no longer an accurate depiction. It means that images conjured up by "lord bishops" who live in palaces might now ring inappropriate if not offensive.

At an even deeper level, this unprecedented transformation of the makeup of the church means that the problems besetting the majority of the world's Anglicans are also different from those faced by Anglicans in such places as the United States, Canada and England. It means that some Anglicans in Northern Nigeria must daily live with the threat of persecution at the hands of their Muslim neighbors.[17] It means that Anglican churches in such places as Uganda and South Africa have learned to break the silence around the HIV-AIDS pandemic, setting up special agencies in their provinces and dioceses to minister to those infected and affected by the AIDS virus and that "AIDS orphanage" has entered the church's lexicon. It means that for the bishop of Colombo, Sri Lanka, the tsunami is a disaster that has come literally to his doorstep, and is not some horrific event half a world away.

"Overseas from Where?" Paradigm Shifts in Global Anglicanism

The further significance of this phenomenon is that, as an Anglican theologian from Hong Kong has observed, "since the Anglican Communion was formed as a direct result of colonization, it is imperative for Anglicans to face the challenges of postcolonial realities."[18] This means that the idea of a church with its headquarters on the banks of the Thames whose outposts dot the globe is an antiquated concept. It is illustrated by the story of an African-American bishop who was in London in 1985 for the consecration of Wilfred Wood, a native of Barbados, as bishop of Croydon. In the vestry of St. Paul's Cathedral, an English bishop approached the black American and asked if he were an "overseas bishop," to which the visiting bishop replied, "Overseas from where?"

If we examine this seemingly innocuous interchange more fully, we see that it is multi-layered. I am indebted to Kortright Davis for providing us with a paradigm for helping us to identify those layers in such a way that we can more fully understand the challenges faced by Anglicanism in the twenty-first century. Professor Davis identifies what he calls "the five cultures of the millennium," namely self-determination, whiteness, technology, materialism and dominance.[19] Davis maintains that the last thousand years has been a story of cultures, often clashing and conflicting, vying for dominance on the world stage. Peoples in every clime, driven by "a struggle for unconditional freedom and rugged individualism," have fought for their rights. Despite "the rise and fall of Afrikaner politics in South Africa" with its "horrible apartheid poison" and other victories, however pyrrhic, of people of color in other places, white racism, according to Davis, is alive and well. The message of the culture of dominance has been that "there are those destined to be in charge and those who are destined to be ruled and governed by others." I believe that at the heart of the issues with which the Anglican Communion is grappling today is a paradigm shift of major proportions, in which the assumptions that power and authority should be in the hands of the "mother church" and her "cousins" in the developed world have been challenged by people of color in the developing world. Such persons, moreover, bring to the table world views born of their cultures and which on their face are at variance with the historically dominant culture. Anglicanism is currently in the throes of sorting this all out.

This paradigm shift has had serious theological and political implications. It means that a theology and an ecclesiastical identity appropriate to the colonial era is deemed inappropriate for a postcolonial era. This is why the South African theologian Luke Pato can express a need for "an authentic African church."[20] This is why Ndungane can speak of a need for an inculturation, indigenization and Africanization of the church, an approach which has effectively replaced an African theology that concentrated on "condemnation of missionary involvement in colonial rule and attitudes of racial superiority and of paternalism."[21] Liberation theologians like James Cone, an African American, and Gustavo Gutierrez, a Peruvian, and their African counterparts such as John Pobee from Ghana and Chukwudum Okolo from Nigeria, have convinced the world that theology looks different when it is written by the underclass, by the "have-nots" of society.[22] In my opening remarks at the second international conference on Afro-Anglicanism,[23] I commented that Anglican theology did not come to an abrupt halt when Hooker's pen ran out of ink.[24]

Anglicans in developing nations no longer see themselves merely as recipients of a Gospel historically used to subjugate and control them. They have, rather, become sowers of the Gospel in their own right, and contenders for the Gospel within a church that has often been inimical or even hostile towards them. Now they have become interpreters of that Gospel, adding their peculiar stamp to that universal enterprise which purports to bring all into Christ's kingdom. It may well be that the Anglican churches in the developed world are, in the words of Mr. Fosdick's hymn, "rich in things and poor in soul."[25] To state the obvious, Anglicans in established churches in the developed world have more money, while Anglicans in developing nations have more people. Recent events would suggest that the latter group are in many cases no longer willing to be unduly intimidated by wealth and the heretofore axiomatic corollary that the church who pays the choir director gets to name the hymns that the people will sing. Instead, recent developments suggest that Anglicans in the two-thirds world are demonstrating that their numbers can be no less an intimidating factor on Anglicanism's world stage.

Finally, the upheaval which has come to Ecclesia Anglicana has serious missiological implications. Questions on the lips of formerly taciturn Anglicans include "Who is missionizing whom?" "Who is bringing the Gospel to whom?" "Which are the sending churches and which the receiving churches?" One of the many missionary hymns written by Reginald Heber (1783–1826), who as bishop of Calcutta counted Southern Africa as part of his vast jurisdiction, was "From Greenland's icy mountains."[26] In it, he issues a challenge to the English missionary eager to reap harvests from a ripe mission field, and boldly asserts, "They call us to deliver their land from error's chain." If the Anglicans of the Global South are singing that hymn today, it is because they see *themselves* as the ones being called—called to deliver those who first brought the Gospel to them from the chains of racism, oppression and today, neocolonialism. Neocolonialism refers to a system in which poor, third-world countries enjoy formal political independence but continue to remain economically dependent on the former colonial power and/or other wealthy, industrialized nations.

Lambeth '08: Business as Usual?

Archbishop Ndungane will not get his wish. An ardent Pan-Africanist, committed to the eradication of every vestige of racism, neocolonialism and imperialism, he had hoped that at the next Lambeth Conference, first-world Anglicans would come to the African continent not in their historical role as missionaries whose purpose was "to correct misperceptions of belief and doctrine and practice," but as fellow pilgrims willing to learn from those beliefs and practices and "to proclaim unity in and through diversity."[27] A Cape Town Lambeth Conference would have been an outward and visible sign of such a development.

Two thousand and eight, therefore, will be a business-as-usual year for the Lambeth Conference, provided, of course, that it takes place.[28] If recent traditions hold, the bishops, in addition to attending their business sessions at the University of Kent, will make pilgrimages to time-honored shrines of English culture. They will attend divine service in the cathedral a few miles away from their campus, erected on the spot where Augustine first brought Christianity to the Angles, and will also worship under Christopher Wren's magnificent dome at St. Paul's Cathedral in London. Their host, the Archbishop of Canterbury, will receive them at luncheon at Lambeth Palace. The Lord Chamberlain, on behalf of Her Majesty the Queen, the head of the Church of England and Defender of the Faith, will invite them to tea on the expansive lawns of Buckingham Palace, where bishops will wear cassocks and their wives will wear hats. (Whether the invitations will include sartorial instructions for bishops' husbands and whether women bishops will be expected to wear cassocks *and* hats remains to be seen.) And their London adventure will be made complete when, to the strains of Handel's "Water Music," the bishops cruise along the Thames on a barge.

Such events suggest that "there will always be an England." The real question is whether there will always be an Anglican Communion as we have come to understand it. It is highly likely that the primate in a developing nation will be the host of an international gathering of Anglican bishops that will be convened after 2008. Some observers opine that there could be a Lambeth XV as well as the initial gathering of a distinct and separate group of Anglicans who may not be in communion with the Archbishop of Canterbury. This issue will undoubtedly be thrashed out during the deliberations in the Kentish countryside in 2008.

In order to more fully appreciate the issues facing Lambeth XIV, including the proposal of Cape Town as a possible venue and the significance of the matters to be discussed there, it will first be necessary to focus on the personage of John William Colenso. One of the most colorful figures in nineteenth century Anglicanism, it was because of his controversial theology and embattled ministry as bishop of Natal that the world's bishops were summoned to the first Lambeth Conference in 1867. Indeed, a study of Bishop Colenso gives us a lens through which we can learn not only about the role of the church in the province of Southern Africa in the history of the Anglican Communion, but about the integral role that the province will play in its future.

Chapter 11

John William Colenso: Anglicanism's Unwitting Architect

Whereas certain of the said extracts [of the writings of Bishop Colenso] do contain opinions, as charged, which contravene and subvert the Catholic Faith as defined and expressed in the Thirty-nine Articles of Religion . . . and certain other extracts do, in substance deprave, impugn and bring into disrepute the Book of Common Prayer, now therefore we do hereby sentence, adjudge, and decree the said Bishop of Natal to be deposed from the said office as such bishop, and to be further prohibited from the exercise of any divine office within any part of the Metropolitical Province of Capetown.

Sentence of Deposition pronounced by Robert Gray, Bishop of Cape Town, following the heresy trial of Bishop Colenso, 16 December 1863

I believe that the kind of cultural sensitivity and openness, which Colenso stood for with all the strength that he had, is a vital ingredient for the church in general and, in particular for the new South Africa. Colenso firmly believed and maintained that salvation was through Jesus Christ and his death on the Cross. Yet he also believed that this work of Christ was freely given for all humankind, whether they knew and accepted it or not. This left him free to recognize the good that there is in other cultures and religions, without having to compromise on his own faith. We need such an attitude and practice in the church today.

—Jonathan A. Draper, Professor of New Testament
University of KwaZulu Natal, Pietermaritzburg[29]

Colenso on Trial

The originally proposed site of the 2008 Lambeth Conference is significant for yet another historic reason, namely that the first Lambeth Conference in 1867 was convened largely because of events that were transpiring in the Church in South Africa at that time. As Archbishop Ndungane stated when he announced his plans to host the Conference in Cape Town, "The first Lambeth Conference was called because of a difference of opinion between the first bishop of Cape Town and the first bishop of Natal; so it would have been a coming home."[30] The Archbishop was referring to the fact that John William Colenso, bishop of Natal, had been deposed by Bishop Gray for heresy, specifically because of his allegedly erroneous biblical teachings and writings. Distressed by the schism that ensued (which, as it turned out, was to consume the energies of the bishops, clergy and people of the South African church for a quarter century), some Canadian bishops petitioned the Archbishop of Canterbury to provide an opportunity for the matter to be considered by the entire Anglican Communion.[31] More than any other event, the Colenso affair served to determine the future course of the Church in South Africa with respect to its theology, polity, spirituality and missionary activity. Moreover, the crisis did much to determine the future course of Anglicanism itself; indeed, Colenso has been called an unwitting architect of the Anglican Communion. For these reasons, it would be helpful to here review the salient events of that celebrated controversy.

Recognizing the impossibility of providing adequate pastoral oversight for his new jurisdiction, encompassing as it did all of Southern Africa under British rule, as well as the island of St. Helena in the Atlantic Ocean, Bishop Gray petitioned the authorities in England to allow him to divide the diocese. In 1853, the sees of Grahamstown and Natal were created, and Colenso was consecrated for the latter. He soon won the reputation of being a firebrand. He was at odds with his dean, the diocesan council, the cathedral chapter and most of his clergy. In 1861, he published *St. Paul's Epistle to the Romans:*

Newly translated, and explained from a missionary point of view, in which he purported to show how he interpreted St. Paul "to the heathen who had never heard the Gospel before." Such a concept, namely that there should be a different method of presenting Holy Scripture to the missionized, was anathema to Colenso's contemporaries. They could not understand that "the history of the missions and the reception of the Bible must be seen as a dialectical process,"[32] and that it might be appropriate, therefore, especially for Colenso, a former lecturer in mathematics at Cambridge, to adapt the pedagogical method to suit the student.

The chief objection to the book, however, was that it asserted, according to Colenso's critics, that the Atonement was an entirely objective event, and that conversion and baptism were, in some sense, meaningless. The missionary's task, according to Colenso, was to assure the heathen that he had already been redeemed. An offending passage from his book read: "The Baptism of a Christian has a meaning and sense, if he walks faithfully; otherwise, his baptism is a nullity. If, then, an unbaptized heathen does that which is good and right and true, shall not his unbaptized state be reckoned for baptism?"

In 1862, Colenso published *The Pentateuch and the Book of Joshua Critically Examined.* It would prove equally objectionable, for in it he challenged the historicity of the text, and applied historical critical method to its reading, which led him to the conclusion that Moses was not the actual author of those books. While such theories would raise few eyebrows today, and would, in most theological circles, not be deemed heretical, Colenso's writings, coming at a time when the conversion of the heathen was of paramount concern to the Anglican Church, caused considerable consternation. Colenso was unwilling to obey Gray's direction that *Romans* be withdrawn from circulation, and in the meantime, two clergymen of the Diocese of Natal had registered formal charges of heresy against their bishop.

Gray then laid the matter before the Archbishop of Canterbury, who in turn called a meeting of thirty-three English, Irish and colonial bishops, who voted to inhibit Colenso from exercising his episcopal office. A second meeting of the bishops demanded that Colenso resign his see, but neither of these actions was enforceable. Moreover, the bishops pointed out that they were incompetent to bring Colenso to trial, since he was "a bishop belonging to a distant jurisdiction." The ball was therefore again in Gray's court, and Colenso was put on trial in Cape Town in November 1863. The court of bishops found

Colenso guilty on nine related charges. Among these were that he maintained that the Bible contained but was not the Word of God; that he denied the authenticity, genuineness, and truth of certain books of the Bible; and, perhaps especially egregious to Anglicans, that he brought parts of the Book of Common Prayer into disrepute. Bishop Gray, exercising the power of his office, (a power which Colenso would later maintain Gray arrogated unto himself) pronounced a sentence of deposition, although in an act of clemency he suspended the sentence until the following April, to give Colenso the opportunity to recant.

Appeals, Reversals and Reversals of Fortune

But the bishop of Natal put the grace period to a different use. As the historiographer of the province of Southern Africa observes: "Beaten on a theological issue, Colenso, with his quick brain, instantly raised a legal one."[33] Undaunted, he appealed to the Privy Council in London.[34] In March, 1865, long after Gray's sentence of deposition took effect, and long after Colenso had returned to England and Gray had declared the see of Natal to be vacant, the Privy Council handed down a ruling which appears convoluted at best to twenty-first century readers. It maintained that the letters patent (i.e., the royal warrant) under which both Gray and Colenso functioned in their respective offices created "ecclesiastical persons" but that those letters could not confer jurisdiction within a colony (such as Natal) that had its own legislature, and that specifically, Gray could have no "coercive jurisdiction" over the bishop of Natal.[35] Both men were recognized as bishops, therefore, but not as bishops *of* anywhere; as a result, Gray could have no jurisdiction over Colenso except by the latter's consent.[36]

The matter was further complicated, it should be noted, by the dates on which the warring bishops assumed their respective sees. Gray's letters patent, as bishop of Cape Town, were issued by the Queen in 1847, but his letters patent as metropolitan were signed on 8 December 1853. Since Colenso's letters patent were issued on 23 November, fifteen days earlier than those of Gray *as metropolitan,* Colenso maintained that Gray had no jurisdiction or authority over him. The Privy Council upheld Colenso's views, and found that Gray's actions against Colenso, therefore, were "null and void."

Thus in the anomalous position of having been vindicated by the Council, yet excommunicated by his putative archbishop, Colenso returned in triumph to his diocese. In a letter to the press, he boasted of his newly clarified status as he understood it:

> In the system of the Church of England, the Queen does ordain—not directly, but virtually—the clergy of all orders, bishops, priests and deacons. What is done by ecclesiastics in this matter is done by them ministerially by virtue of power committed to them by the Queen, I mean, as representing the State—the people.[37]

Colenso's protests notwithstanding, Gray persevered in his search for a new bishop for the diocese. When consecrated, the new bishop, W. K. Macrorie, as bishop of Maritzburg,[38] and Colenso, as bishop of Natal, had overlapping jurisdictions, each with his own cathedral, but Macrorie ministered to members of "the Church of South Africa in Natal," while Colenso had the pastoral charge of a small but faithful band of followers who styled themselves "the Church of England in Natal." To further complicate matters, the Privy Council had awarded to Colenso the control of church property.

It was in the midst of this unprecedented muddle in church governance (Macrorie accepted the election to Maritzburg in 1867 but wasn't consecrated until two years later) that the first Lambeth Conference took place. In his response to the request from the Canadian bishops, Archbishop Charles Thomas Longley wrote that he looked forward to meeting together, to "take such counsel and adopt such measures, as may be best fitted to provide for the present distress." He added, "I can well understand your surprise and alarm at the recent decisions of the . . . Privy Council in grave matters bearing upon the doctrine and discipline of our Church." Seventy-six bishops (out of 144 who were invited) were in attendance.[39] Fifty-six of them signed a resolution accepting "the sentence pronounced upon Dr. Colenso by the Metropolitan of South Africa and his Suffragans, as being a spiritually valid sentence."[40] And although there was an agreement among the bishops present that no specific mention would be made of Colenso, Bishop Selwyn of New Zealand moved a resolution that the whole church was injured by the situation in Natal, and John Hopkins, the presiding bishop of the Episcopal Church, called for Colenso's excommunication.[41]

But the bishops were not content to commiserate and pass judgment. In an effort to preclude the possibility of another situation analogous to that of Natal, the bishops passed a resolution, put forward by Bishop Selwyn, "that in the opinion of this conference unity of faith and discipline will be best maintained among the several branches of the Anglican Communion by due and canonical subordination of the synods of the several branches to the higher authority of a synod or synods above them."[42] This resolution was skillfully worded, even in its lack of specificity, to allow for diocesan and provincial conferences as well as a Lambeth Conference, but made no provision for a higher synod or court of appeal such as the Privy Council which could interfere in church matters. Steps were later taken in committee to implement this resolution, "which became so important in the work of building up the present system of independent provinces in communion with one another."[43] These decisions of the Lambeth Conference, as we shall see, are especially germane to the issues currently facing the Anglican Communion.

Colenso's Legacy

What did Bishop Colenso bequeath to the church? First, it would appear that to his fellow bishops, Colenso's greater sin was his Erastianism, not his heresy. His biographer explains that

> an Erastian is one who believes as a matter of theological principle that the State *ought* to control and exercise all jurisdiction in the Church. Erastianism is not just a vague feeling that the Church ought to be established. It is a *belief* that all ecclesiastical authority flows from God through the State.[44]

The promulgation of Colenso's views wreaked havoc in the Church in South Africa and was a serious threat to its missionary enterprise. Such theological opinions might have been tolerated had Colenso been a simple country parson, but his episcopal office gave them weight. Edward Pusey, the Anglo-Catholic don at Oxford who was one of the pioneers of the Oxford movement, commented, "If he were still *Mr.* Colenso, his book would have been still-born. His book is read by tens of thousands because he is a Bishop. It is his office of Bishop which propagates infidelity."[45] As to his lesser sin, few biblical scholars today would label Colenso a heretic. Indeed, "the Anglican Church has changed its position regarding the bishop's orthodoxy,"[46] and most theologians would maintain that his approach to biblical criticism was simply ahead of its time. Indeed, the recently retired bishop of Natal credits his early predecessor for having been a pioneer in freedom of thought, whose "controversial developments in biblical thought have become commonplace today."[47] Jonathan Draper, an expert on Colenso, concurs, asserting that "Colenso's interpretation of Scripture sounds today no different from what is taught at many theological colleges."[48]

While such views on Colenso's approach to the Bible are widespread, the jury is still out on his orthodoxy as it applies to his understanding of the person of Jesus Christ. As Bishop Nuttall remarked, "The issue is not his biblical criticism; the world has come to accept his views, by and large. The real question is his Christology. He leaned toward diminishing the role of Jesus the Son. He even disallowed hymns that addressed the second person of the Trinity."[49] Archbishop Ndungane expressed a similar opinion: "The major issue with Colenso," he observed, "was not his commitment to indigenization; it was his views on the divinity of Jesus."[50] It can be argued that Colenso fashioned a Jesus to fit his missiology. Since he believed that it was not the purpose of the missionary "to save a few souls from everlasting burnings" but "to raise the whole race to the true dignity of man,"[51] it was more important that Jesus be seen "as an example of the love of God, as a teacher, and not as vicarious savior."[52] His defective Christology was in many ways a consequence of his more enlightened missiology.

The Question of Exculpation

Colenso, who has been on the theological radar screen in recent years owing to the observance, in 2003, of the 150th anniversary of his consecration as bishop of Natal, has benefited from a 21st century view of justice. This, combined with a belief that Colenso's trial was in many ways flawed,[53] led the Provincial Synod of the CPSA in 2002, upon motion made by Bishop Philip Rubin of Natal, to vote by an overwhelming majority to recommend, in principle, that the excommunication of Colenso on the grounds of heresy be lifted. Bishop Rubin's motion described Colenso as a man of integrity, devoted to understanding Zulu language and culture. It stated that Colenso's theology, "though radical for his day, may not have transcended the bounds of what today would be considered acceptable theological diversity, and has in many respects been vindicated by recent understandings and trends in theology and biblical study." Accordingly, the resolution declared that its mover "would wholeheartedly support a rescission of Colenso's excommunication, should the Synod of Bishops so decide." It further requested that the Archbishop lay the matter before that House, whose members, "in light of our new understanding," would implement a process needed to effect the rescinding of the excommunication.[54]

This was more easily said than done. Bishop Nuttall commented that while it sounds like a good idea, it is something that has little precedent, adding, "The Church must live with her mistakes." Archbishop Ndungane observed that the problem with the exculpation of an individual is that someone else must, of necessity, be found blameworthy. Draper, on the other hand, is unequivocal on the matter of where blame should be laid: "In this particular matter of the mission of Colenso and his trial for heresy, Gray quite simply made a grievous mistake and error of judgment and the church should not try and cover it up. The church should be capable of admitting its fallibility and its mistakes."[55]

Some South African Anglicans even further opined that given that the first Lambeth Conference took place largely because of the Colenso affair, and then upheld the verdict against him, that the fourteenth Lambeth Conference would be the appropriate venue for reconsideration of the charges. But this seems especially unlikely, not only because of the change of venue of the Conference, but because the resolution presented at Synod was referred to a committee of the House of Bishops of the province who would seek legal and theological expertise before proceeding, but to date no action has been taken.

In the meantime, however, Colenso has been honored in a way which may turn out to be a more lasting and more fitting legacy. In describing the CPSA's Anglican Prayer Book 1989, Bishop Nuttall writes:

> A theologically liberal outlook, strongly represented during the early history of the Anglican Church in Southern Africa in the writings and utterances of the prophetic and controversial first bishop of Natal, John William Colenso, is neatly and intriguingly contained in the Word of God section of the Eucharist.

Nuttall goes on to explain that the lector now says at the end of the lesson: "Hear the word of the Lord," and not "This is the word of the Lord." The new words imply that the listener may weigh what has been read and discern the spiritual truth within it. "The new wording thus allows for the belief that the Bible is the place where we may hear the word of God without holding that in every respect it is literally the word of God."[56] Considering that one of the charges laid against Colenso in his heresy trial was that he held that the Bible contained the word of God but was not the word of God, it would appear that the deposed bishop has received a de facto exculpation by means of a Prayer Book rubric, as opposed to synodical legislation. In a church whose Prayer Book also functions as its systematic theology, this may prove to be the greater pardon.

Indigenization of the Gospel

There was, admittedly, a deeper issue inherent in the charges against Colenso—namely that he "advocated revolutionary and unpopular missionary policies" and "asserted very firmly that the Christian gospel possessed definite social implications."[57] In other words, Colenso's missiology was seriously at odds with the prevailing view of the Church of England. He believed that the way forward for the church was not, as was the expectation of English missionaries, for new converts summarily to reject African religious traditions and customs, but, as one South African historian has described it, "to leaven African culture and its social system with the gospel."[58] Colenso recognized the intrinsic worth of the African, and more specifically "in the full humanity of the Zulu people he was to pastor as bishop."[59] He did not agree, therefore, that the waters of Baptism were intended to wash away the "grime" of African cultural identity and heritage. On this point, Colenso and his erstwhile friend, Bishop Gray, were diametrically opposed.[60]

Colenso's theology of mission was far ahead of his time. While most nineteenth-century Christian missionaries "left home with a social universe which appeared self-evident, secure and superior to the indigenous cultures and beliefs of the colonized peoples," Colenso espoused a sensitivity to and respect for the culture of those to whom the Gospel was introduced, and saw the African people not as "mere passive victims of European aggression, but purposive participants in events."[61] He was a firm believer, as one of his biographers described it, that "missionary endeavor had to be based on the interchange and not the imposition of ideas."[62]

While today such attitudes are expected of missionaries, they were nothing short of scandalous to Colenso's contemporaries, within and without the church. Even Benjamin Disraeli, in a famous speech delivered in Oxford in 1864, made a not too veiled allusion to Colenso when he spoke of "the cruder conclusions of prelates who appear to have commenced their theological studies after they had grasped the crozier, and who introduce to society their obsolete discoveries with the startling wonder and frank ingenuousness of their own savages."[63] The Prime Minister and others could not conceive of a bishop like Colenso who "approached his missionary task not in a triumphalist or pietistic manner, but more with a view to touching the hearts and minds of the converts in such a way that they should own it fully."[64]

Modern missiological scholarship has caught up with Colenso. A recent statement issued by the Mission Commission of the Anglican Communion recognized that "in mission history the gospel has too often been identified with the culture of the missionary," and admitted that "only in this century has our Communion begun to learn how to distinguish Anglo-Saxonism from Anglicanism. The Gospel is not only a transforming challenge to human culture, but also to the Church itself."[65]

Colenso and the Zulus

The province of Natal was and is the land of the Zulu nation, and the Zulus have long been a powerful and important people in Southern Africa. Shortly after his arrival in Natal in 1854, Colenso immersed himself in the study of the Zulu language, and wrote a Zulu grammar and a Zulu-English dictionary. Through these means, he identified with and endeared himself to the people he served, so much so that the Zulus called him *Sobantu,* "father of the people." He would later champion the cause of the natives against Boer oppression and write books in which he advocated for Zulus who were mistreated by English colonialists. It is noteworthy that in 2000, the city of Umsunduzi honored Colenso by adding his name to the Civic Honours Register along with the names of heroes who in a more recent liberation struggle fought against apartheid.[66]

Colenso's views on polygamy provide us with a deeper understanding of his defense of Zulu culture. The prevalent view in his day was that the convert was required to give up all but one of his wives upon conversion, even if that meant that the discarded wives would be ostracized and subject to a life of penury and shame for herself and her children. Such a view was upheld by the Lambeth Conference of 1888, over the pleadings of the sole African bishop in attendance, Samuel Crowther of Nigeria. The Conference affirmed that polygamy was inconsistent with the law of Christ respecting marriage, and reported that it was better to withhold baptism from polygamous persons until they accepted the law of Christ. Such views ran afoul of Colenso's view of justice. In a hundred-page letter to the Archbishop of Canterbury, entitled "Letter to His Grace the Archbishop of Canterbury upon the Question of the Proper Treatment of Cases of Polygamy, as Found Already Existing in Converts from Heathenism," he contended that many pious men of the Old Testament were polygamous and that the lascivious David was "a man after God's own heart." Moreover, observing that Jesus, while condemning divorce, was silent on the matter of polygamy, he argued that Zulus should be accorded some degree of understanding and compassion. "It was Colenso's ardent wish that the Anglican Church should work out guidelines under which polygamous people may be baptized and become full members of the Church."[67]

It would take nearly a century and a half for Colenso's wish to be granted. Rescinding the actions of the 1888 Conference, Resolution 26 of the XII Lambeth Conference of 1988 declared that a polygamist "who responds to the Gospel who wishes to join the Anglican Church may be baptized and confirmed." One of the conditions is that "the polygamist shall not be compelled to put away any of his wives on account of the social deprivation they would suffer."

Unwitting Architect

That said, the extent of Colenso's legacy was one that he could not have foreseen. History has shown that church councils are born of controversy. Since Nicaea, beliefs deemed incompatible with church doctrine and polity have been grist for conciliar mills. The hope is that the council's grind will yield a pure, doctrinal wheat, free of tares. The first Lambeth Conference was no exception. The difficulties which John William Colenso laid at the Lambeth Palace door forced his fellow bishops inside to grapple with them, and as a result, the bishops developed a system of governance for the Anglican Communion which, with some modifications, has lasted to this day. In this regard, it is important to note that when Gray's successor, William West Jones, was consecrated in Westminster Abbey, he signed a document recognizing the

Archbishop of Canterbury as "first place among all the prelates of the Anglican Communion," but having no jurisdiction in the Province of South Africa, except such as the constitution of the province might give him.[68] This principle, cherished by the bishops and the first and second Lambeth Conferences, has been, as we shall see, ignored with impunity in recent pronouncements by Anglican primates. Secondly, the Colenso controversy helped to establish a tradition of a decennial conference of Anglican bishops, which now prepares for its fourteenth meeting. Clearly, the seventy-six bishops assembled at Lambeth in 1867 believed, rightly as it turned out, that there would be an ongoing need for bishops to meet from time to time for "brotherly (and now sisterly) counsel."

It is not enough, therefore, to state that the first Lambeth Conference happened to come into being as the result of a dispute in the South African church. On the global level, the Colenso controversy helped to determine the future shape of the Anglican Communion and the role of the Lambeth Conference as arbiter. The resolution of the Colenso controversy with respect to the authority of bishops led to the Anglican concept of provincial autonomy, a matter which is at the heart of the current controversies in the Communion. Colenso's views of Scripture for which he was brought to trial later proved normative for Anglican thought. Colenso's penchant for respecting the cultural realities of those to whom the Gospel is brought has paved the way for a more progressive approach to mission. His plea for compassion toward polygamous Zulus set the stage not only for Lambeth's rescission of stringent anti-polygamy laws, but raised the question of whether the church should recognize relationships other than heterosexual monogamy. Within South Africa, Colenso's actions did much to engender a tolerance for differences within church and society.

As we look at the South African church today as an example of forbearance and a model for the Communion, we must remember that the CPSA is largely indebted to Colenso for learning to live in tension, and no less indebted to him for blazing a path for the Anglican Communion to follow. The Church in South Africa has never lost sight of that role; nor has there been a time in the history of the Communion when such an approach to Anglicanism has been more needed.

Chapter III

A Glimpse of the Heavenly Jerusalem: Anglo-Catholicism and Social Witness in the CPSA

Authentic Anglican spirituality is catholic and so it is eucharistic and incarnational. . . . We are bidden to ascend to the mount of transfiguration not to remain there forever but to be inspired by the divine vision to descend into the valley of human need and crass stupidity and incomprehension as agents of transfiguration to help God achieve His goal so that . . . those who having found Christ in the Mass . . . will go out to find Him in the lanes and streets of our ghettoes, to wash His feet and to minister to Him in the downtrodden."

—Archbishop Desmond Tutu[69]

The Vision of a Whole Society Redeemed

It would be misleading to suggest that Bishop Colenso's particular approach to mission, characterized, as it was, by a special sensitivity to the indigenous population, stood in stark contrast to a paternalistic and uncaring attitude on the part of other missionaries. We have seen how Colenso, an Evangelical churchman, affected the life of the South African church. To make the picture complete, and to understand something of the theological and sociopolitical identity of the South African church, we must also appreciate the debt that it owes to the Anglo-Catholic movement.

In some circles, "Anglo-Catholic" and "high church" are pejorative terms, which conjure up an image of clergy and people preoccupied with the externals ("the bells and smells") of worship. Implicit in such a disingenuous characterization is the suggestion that Anglo-Catholics have no interests or concerns—pastoral, theological, or social—beyond such liturgical minutiae. Men like John Henry Newman, Edward Bouverie Pusey and John Keble, who were at the forefront of the catholic revival in the 1830's, which became known as the Oxford Movement, would be surprised to learn that such a perception of their valiant witness is part of their legacy. Vestments, incense and elaborate ceremony were concerns that were at best ancillary to the primary foci of the Movement. "Newman himself was indifferent to them; Pusey hostile. . . . The Tractarians were concerned with invisible, not visible things."[70] Among those invisible things were theology, ecclesiology, and social action.

The theology of the Oxford Movement, on which so much else depends, is probably its greatest gift to the church. The Anglican apologist P. E. More noted that "the Oxford Movement brought theology back to the path from which it had deviated in the arid intervening years," namely between the seventeenth and nineteenth centuries.[71] The Tractarians (so named because they published *Tracts for the Times,* a series of pamphlets which systematically outlined the theology and rationale of the Movement) built on the concept of the *via media* (or "middle way") as espoused by seventeenth-century divines such as Richard Hooker, Jeremy Taylor and Lancelot Andrewes, and made it central to their teaching. As one theologian described it, in the Oxford Movement, "the Via Media became a glorious reality instead of a barren philosophical theory."[72] The Anglican Church, in many ways a consequence of the Elizabethan Settlement,[73] had long been seen as the via media.

Such an understanding of Anglicanism emerged in response to two related dangers. The first was political—the threat of the intervention of the Roman Church in the temporal affairs of nations on the one hand, and the Calvinist theory of state which curtailed the independence of the church on the other. The second danger was theological. The Anglican method, which by its nature is given to eschewing extremes, was seen as a way to avoid the encroachment of either Catholic tradition as the defining norm for the church or conversely the imposition of the deficient Calvinist doctrine of *sola scriptura.* It is important, however, to perceive the via media not as a "path between," but as a "bridge across." The Anglican genius is "the sense that it attempts to be inclusive rather than exclusive in its theologizing."[74] That genius is perhaps nowhere better expressed than in the ordinal. The bishop's words pronounced at the ordination of priests make clear the all-encompassing role of the presbyter: As the Bible is delivered into the priest's hand, the bishop says, "Be thou a faithful dispenser of the Word of God and of his holy sacraments."[75]

The via media embraced the idea of Hooker's so-called "three-legged stool" of Scripture, tradition and reason.[76] The last of these is of particular significance. What distinguished the Oxford Movement from other religious movements was the scholarship of its founders. "The Tractarians," as one historian has commented, "possessed all the moral earnestness and religious emotion of the Evangelicals; but combined them with an intellectual power of analysis and exposition, to a degree long unknown in England."[77]

The doctrine of the church as espoused by the Tractarians posited what would prove to be a radical and counter-cultural hypothesis for Victorian England. In the first instance, the Oxford divines maintained that the Church of England was not an invention of the Reformation, but was an integral part of the undivided pre-Reformation Church, which had its roots in antiquity and could trace its origins to the apostles themselves. For this reason, the Oxford divines appealed in their theological arguments to the early church fathers, such as Athanasius, Cyprian and Tertullian. Thus, Newman believed that the Oxford Movement was the means through which the religion of the primitive church was conveyed, through Anglican formularies and Anglican divines, to the Church of England in the nineteenth century.[78]

Believing, too, that the church was the direct consequence of the Incarnation, the Oxford divines contended that the Church of England was compromised and inhibited because of its established status, and therefore was in danger of losing its identity, indeed its very soul. As the church historian Moorman has observed, the Oxford apostles believed that "for too long the church had been looked on, by the majority of its members, as little more than a department of State, the religious aspect of the national life."[79]

So central was their high doctrine of the church to the catholic revival that the Oxford Movement is often said to have been inaugurated by John Keble's famous Assize Sermon, preached in the University Church of St. Mary the Virgin, Oxford, on 14 July 1833. It embodied a protest against Parliament, which had recently done away with—that is, confiscated the endowments of— half of the dioceses in the Anglican Church in Ireland. Keble, who justifiably believed that bishoprics in England would likely be the next to suffer a similar fate, maintained that the acts of Parliament amounted to "a rejection of a national profession of religion," or a "National Apostasy," which, indeed, became the name by which the sermon would be known. The church, Keble maintained, possessed, by divine law, the right of uninterrupted succession as the Apostolic Church in England, and to deprive her of her worldly goods was tantamount to an act of sacrilege.

Tractarian Influence on the South African Church

These developments are crucial to the understanding of the South African church, for they speak to the Tractarians' inherent distrust of Erastianism and their belief that, unchecked, it would result in a situation in which the church would be entirely deprived of its freedom to act as a prophetic agent. As we shall see, the church deemed it necessary to be seen as a separate and distinct entity, in order that it would be free to challenge the state when necessary. The work of the Gospel would be impeded by Erastianism, an issue central to the Colenso controversy, since it would so strongly "emphasize the connection of Church and state, that it entirely loses sight of the church's supernatural and spiritual reality."[80]

Robert Gray, the first bishop of Cape Town, had been a student at Oxford when the ideas of the Oxford Movement were in their formative stages, and was influenced by the catholic revival. By the time he was a young parish priest in the diocese of Durham, he had read the *Tracts* and "declared himself much pleased."[81] He was an unabashed high churchman, insofar as he subscribed to the idea that the church was of divine origin, and should enjoy an existence independent of secular influence. Gray's insistence that the church in South Africa be self-governing and independent, yet *in full communion with the Church of England*, as well as his belief that the church there must be both "primitive and apostolic" were consonant with the Anglo-Catholic principle that the church is the primary sacrament. He refused to conform to the expectation that he function merely as a colonial chaplain, doing the Queen's bidding in a territorial outpost. He believed that the exigencies of the Diocese of Cape Town could not be compared, say, to Bristol (where his father and namesake had been bishop). If he was to execute his duties effectively, he found it necessary to be given free rein.

If we are to comprehend the Anglo-Catholic influence on the South African church, we must fathom the social ramifications of the Oxford Movement. The social action which was a manifestation and outgrowth of the Movement, which was influenced in no small measure by the Christian Socialism of Frederick Denison Maurice and William Temple, had "a two-fold foundation: the doctrine of the incarnation and a mystical identification with the poor."[82] The Anglo-Catholic ethos demanded a growth toward sanctity, displayed, ideally, in a life of humility and self-sacrifice, obedience and holiness. Such a life, predicated as it was on the belief in the real presence of Christ in the Eucharist, was to be lived out in a sociopolitical context. This led, in turn, in many cases, to an increasing commitment by Anglo-Catholic clergy and religious to live among and serve the poor. Indeed, as Hinchliff has observed, "the ideal of the priest became that of the Christian socialist, struggling to bring the Faith to the poor and underprivileged, fighting their battles in matters of housing, of political and civil rights, striving for social justice, fair wages and sweated labor."[83]

The Oxford Movement, then, while it had its intellectual genesis in an Oxford common room, lived out its incarnational reality in the London slums, where Anglo-Catholic priests served the working classes at a time when the Church of England ministered by and large only to the middle and upper classes. The late bishop Paul Moore described those clergy as "incarnational, sacramental Catholics, living out the gospel with the Christ of the altar and the Christ of the poor."[84] The very word "catholic" is from the Greek *kath' olon,* "according to the whole," and Anglo-Catholics cherished the idea that the Gospel was intended for all of God's children: "They were captured by the haunting and perplexing vision of a whole society redeemed, not just individuals within it. . . . So the doctrine of the Incarnation led them to the dispossessed and it filled some of them with visions of a transformed society, become God's kingdom on earth."[85]

Bishop Gray's "high" theology of the Church, as evidenced in his own writings and teachings, as well as in the resolution of the Colenso affair, served to earn for South Africa a reputation of being a "catholic" province, and for that reason, "the clergy recruited for service in the province came from Anglo-Catholic strongholds in England."[86] This reputation was earned because Gray was perceived as a staunch defender of the catholic (and Anglican) principle of church government by bishops against the Protestant (and, ironically, no less Anglican) idea of the supremacy of private judgment in religion. The theology, ecclesiology and personal piety of the Anglo-Catholics gave them a fierce independence, which has proved ideally suited to the task which the church in South Africa has undertaken for more than a hundred and fifty years—confronting injustice and oppression. This is not to suggest that the CPSA has had an unblemished record in this regard. Nevertheless, a spirit of protest coupled with a commitment to advocacy for the downtrodden, have long characterized the work of the South African church.

The Work of the Religious Orders

One of the Oxford Movement's most significant contributions to the life of the CPSA has been its influence through the ministry of the religious orders which came to South Africa beginning in the latter part of the nineteenth century. The revival of the religious life was one of the fruits of the Oxford Movement, and several Anglican communities were founded in England. Members of such monastic orders came to South Africa in great numbers, and worked in parishes, hospitals, schools and seminaries. Having taken vows of poverty, chastity and obedience, they were virtually free of all worldly encumbrances, and were able to offer themselves wholly to the service of the people of the province. They brought both talent and devotion to their work, and were especially helpful to the struggling South African church, since they received no payment for their considerable labors.

Among the orders which had significant work in South Africa have been the Society of St. Augustine, the Society of St. John the Baptist, the Community of St. Mary the Virgin (the Wantage Sisters); the Society of St. Mary of the Cross, the Society of the Sacred Mission (the Kelham Fathers) and the Society of St. John the Evangelist (the Cowley Fathers). The Cowley Fathers had been invited to South Africa by Bishop Gray, but they didn't arrive until 1885, eleven years after the bishop's death. At least two orders were founded in South Africa—the Community of St. Michael and All Angels, and the Society of St. John the Divine. Several clergy and at least three bishops of the province, notably Archbishop Robert Selby Taylor, have been members of a non-residential religious community, the Oratory of the Good Shepherd, which described itself as "a society of celibate priests and laymen of the Anglican Communion . . . to live a life of devotion and service."[87] Still other bishops and clergy, including Desmond Tutu, have been tertiaries of religious orders, those who seek to live by the rule of a religious order adapted to life in the world.

The Community of the Resurrection (the Mirfield Fathers) deserves special mention. It was founded in 1892 by six parish priests who saw as their vocation a ministry to the working poor in the north of England. In 1903, several members of the order responded to a request from the bishop of Pretoria to come to South Africa. Their members exercised a significant ministry in the province, as parish priests, teachers and bishops. They also became known for their dedicated ministry to miners, working in compounds through which a stream of men from all over South Africa constantly passed. Through this effort, they were able to do much to raise the consciousness of the public about the adverse conditions under which the miners were forced to work. Indeed, the plight of the miners had become emblematic of the inequity of apartheid. Black miners, on whose backs South Africa became rich, worked for paltry wages (one of the grievances of the celebrated miners' strike in 1946 was their monthly wage of four pounds, one twelfth that of white miners). To make matters worse, the workers, miles away from the townships in which their families resided, were forced to live in crowded hostels, an environment which left the men especially susceptible to tuberculosis.[88] The Mirfield Fathers stood in solidarity with the strikers, and Geoffrey Clayton, bishop of Johannesburg, later visitor to the Order, "roundly condemned the dictatorial handling of the miners' strike" and the violence and bloodshed it brought about.[89]

In addition to founding more than forty schools, the Mirfield Fathers, believing that "the chief agents in evangelization must be the Africans themselves and their training one of our major tasks,"[90] also served as the faculty of St. Peter's College, Rosettenville, where Desmond Tutu trained for the ordained ministry.[91] Tutu's biographer points out, however, that the CR fathers did more than provide academic training for the future archbishop. "It is in Desmond Tutu's spirituality that the legacy of St. Peter's and the Community of the Resurrection can principally be seen. The regimen of spiritual practice that the CR fathers modeled became central to his daily life" and ministry. His spirituality is "prayerful, Gospel-centered, prophetic, disciplined and catholic minded."[92]

The influence of the Mirfield Fathers on the leadership of the South African church has been extremely significant. Even today, many of the black clergy in South Africa can claim to have received their theological education from the Mirfield Fathers.[93] A priest of the order commented that perhaps the only "blessing" of the apartheid era was that because the government's housing policies precluded the possibility of whites living in black areas, it provided a pressing need for the raising up of black vocations, a need to which the Fathers happily responded. It should be added that priestly vocations were not the only ones that were fostered. Father Trevor Huddleston gave one of his altar boys his first trumpet. His name was Hugh Masakela, and he became South Africa's most famous jazz musician!

One of the founders of the order was the distinguished Anglo-Catholic biblical scholar, Charles Gore, later bishop of Oxford. Remarkably, one of his essays in *Lux Mundi, A Series of Studies in the Religion of the Incarnation,* which he edited, was entitled "The Holy Spirit and Inspiration," which adopted most of the essentials of Colenso's biblical theology, not the least of which were contextualization of the Gospel message and its indigenization. (Unfortunately, the excommunicated bishop of Natal had been dead for eight years, and never learned that his views had become widely respected.) Thus, St. Peter's, Rosettenville, whose library was liberally sprinkled with Gore's work, became a center of biblical criticism, and by extension, a social Gospel, with its emphasis on the relation of faith to justice. It was this setting in which a black consciousness was steadily developing. It was here that Trevor Huddleston, who saw in the story of the Exodus a paradigm for South African struggle, wrote his famous memoir, *Naught for Your Comfort,* which chronicles his relentless campaign against apartheid.

Although not all church leaders were associated with religious orders, the orders' spirit of dedication and self-sacrifice, hallmarks of monastic life, seemed to infuse itself into the work of the South African church. The incarnational reality of the Anglo-Catholic ethos demanded that such dedication and self-sacrifice be translated into action. The focus of that action has changed. Archbishop Ndungane points out whereas religious communities in the past concentrated on education and "works of mercy," the eleven orders currently active in the CPSA are working "towards evangelism, counseling and deepening the life of prayer and witness."[94]

Archbishop Tutu cited another way in which the Anglo-Catholic ethos in general and the presence of religious orders in particular affected life in the province:

First of all, we stand on the shoulders of men like Huddleston, Reeves, deBlank and Clayton, all of whom were grounded in spirituality. What is more, our synods were always grounded in prayer, and we began each day with the holy eucharist. And there were always members of the religious communities, in their habits, present at Synod, as a visible reminder that there were people in our midst who saw it as one of their primary responsibilities to pray for all of us in the Diocese. It has always added to our sense of wholeness.[95]

"Going into the highways and the hedges"

Tutu's sense of wholeness is central to the understanding of the church in South Africa. Wholeness, of course, is the literal meaning of catholicity. The catholic ethos is, by definition, all-embracing. A catholic church can recognize no classes of membership; nor can it exclude any from its midst. In describing Desmond Tutu's theology of the church, Michael Battle writes: "The miracle of the church is that everyone—the poor, the rich, the free, the slave, male, female, black, white—can find one identity in Christ."[96] But the church is not, in any event, a club-like institution which screens and vets applicants, finding them worthy or unworthy of belonging. The church is by nature a missionary institution, described by Archbishop William Temple as the only organization whose primary obligation is to benefit those *not* its members. Of all the parables about the Kingdom of God, Jesus' story about the dragnet (Matt 13:47–50) is perhaps the most descriptive of the church. The dragnet is indiscriminate; it catches every species of fish in its draw. And Jesus is quick to remind us that sorting out and separating good fish from bad is not the function of us as fishers of people, but of the angels at the end of the age.

The Anglican Church in South Africa has historically been a community with such a self-understanding. Thus, Bishop Colenso through his universalist theology manifested the highest of catholic principles in his ministry to the Zulus and in his attempt to welcome them into the fellowship of Christ's religion without a demand that they forsake their cultural identity. Unlike many of his contemporaries, Colenso recognized that English culture was not part and parcel of the missionary enterprise. It is easy to understand, therefore, how, later in its existence, a church grounded in catholic principles would oppose apartheid. For church leaders, that system was not just a government-imposed practice of discrimination. It was sin, since it denied the unalienable rights of individuals as children of God, declaring some of those children to be of lesser worth than others, a sin made the more egregious since the government used Holy Scripture as justification for its practices.

Two other aspects of the Anglo-Catholic ethos played an important role in the church's life in South Africa. The first was a belief in the Incarnation. "Behind all the visible and audible protests of the Oxford Apostles," writes Father England, "stood the primary sacrament, namely the church, and silhouetted behind its concreteness was the God-man and the doctrine of the Incarnation."[97] Such a belief in the Incarnation erases the line between sacred and secular. Everything is sacred because it is redeemed by the fact of Jesus' taking on human flesh and living among mortals. A consequence of this basic Christian truth is that there is no arena into which the church cannot legitimately enter. The church, therefore, in the name of Christ, can oppose the government, raise questions about political practices, and wade into society's troubled waters with impunity. "The belief that God became man in Jesus Christ inspired many to serve in the slums and among the poor, exploited and oppressed in the Province."[98]

The other aspect of the Anglo-Catholic ethos is the sense of the holy, the numinous. Rich and elaborate liturgical practices were not spectacles performed for an audience, but the offering of worship to Almighty God in an attempt to capture a glimpse of the heavenly Jerusalem here on earth. In its worship, then, the church offers splendor instead of squalor, grandeur instead of degradation, dignity instead of indignity, awesomeness instead of awfulness. But, importantly, the theology of such worship did not allow it to be limited to rites and ceremonies carried out within the confines of church buildings. It was from the altar that priest and people derived the strength to go out into the world to render service. The priestly hand raised in blessing could also be seen raised in a power salute at an anti-apartheid rally. The feet of the faithful might one day be walking in a procession, and the next be marching in a demonstration on behalf of the victims of Sharpeville massacre. Canon Paterson develops this theme even further. Believing that the liturgy "is a powerful vehicle through which liberation from oppression can be expressed," worship, especially among black South Africans, contains both "extreme solemnity and formality" as well as "gay abandon and expressions of deep anguish." It can become, in this way, "an objectification of the community's experiences and hopes."[99]

Espousing such a theology of worship, therefore, catholic Christians in the CPSA were obedient to the celebrated charge of Frank Weston, bishop of Zanzibar, in an address entitled "Our Present Duty," delivered at the Anglo-Catholic Congress in London in 1923. Admonishing the delegates that "it is folly—it is madness—to suppose that you can worship Jesus in the Sacraments and Jesus on the Throne of glory, when you are sweating him in the souls and bodies of his children," he ended his speech with these stirring words: "You have got your Mass, you have got your Altar, you have begun to get your Tabernacle. Now go out into the highways and hedges where not even the Bishops will try to hinder you. Go out and look for Jesus in the ragged, in the naked, in the oppressed and sweated, in those who have lost hope, in those who are struggling to make good. Look for Jesus. And when you see him, gird yourselves with his towel and try to wash their feet."

Bishop Weston's charge served as a summons to the South African church. Her people did not have to look far to find the ragged, the naked and the oppressed. They were not only at the church's doorsteps, they were within her precincts. Nor did the church have to search far and wide to identify the source of the people's oppression, or the reason that so many of them had lost hope. The invidious system of apartheid was predicated on a distortion of the message of the Gospel and was used to subjugate the people of God and to justify depriving them of God-given rights. Apartheid, reinforced by government policy and an intricate and tyrannical system of laws, had created a class of persons, who, because of the color of their skin, were separated from the mainstream. They became in effect an underclass, cut off from the sources of economic support that others took for granted.

The church could not countenance apartheid because it was so clearly inimical to her most fundamental beliefs. In the second half of the twentieth century, therefore, most members of the Christian community in South Africa, the Anglican Church at the helm, took to heart Mary's words. They set about to "put down the mighty from their seats and exalt the humble and meek." The war for racial justice was engaged, with Church and state on opposing sides of the battlefield. The church, if true to herself, could not defend a position of neutrality. Swords were drawn, and bishops, accustomed to carrying a shepherd's crook, soon found themselves cast in the role of gladiator.

Chapter IV

From Paternalism to Activism: The South African Church and Racial Justice

I believe that, because God became Man, therefore human nature in itself has a dignity and a value which is infinite. I believe that this conception necessarily carries with it the idea that the State exists for the individual, not the individual for the State. Any doctrine based on racial or colour prejudice and enforced by the State is therefore an affront to human dignity and 'ipso facto' an insult to God himself. It is for this reason that I feel bound to oppose not only the policy of the present Government of the Union of South Africa but the legislation which flows from this policy.

—Trevor Huddleston, CR

Fits and Starts

It would be naïve to suggest that the CPSA from its founding has been an unswerving champion of racial justice, especially as we would understand the term today. Michael Battle observes that while the Anglican Church in South Africa could not always claim to be a forerunner in this arena, "it carried within itself the impulses for protest."[100] When in the mid-nineteenth century colonial and missionary expansion was undertaken in earnest, it was characterized by a marked paternalism. "Britons were convinced of their ability to bring liberation and light to what they regarded as the Dark Continent,"[101] but such liberation was deemed to be emancipation from the shackles of heathenism, not from an oppression which was the step-child of race and class prejudice.

English missionaries of the period, Colenso being one of the few exceptions, believed that African culture and religion, not being British in origin, were of no value. Archbishop Tutu once observed in a sermon that missionaries "thought European was synonymous with being Christian. . . They often made our people shamed of being African [and] often destroyed our rich cultural traditions."[102] British prosperity in the post-Industrial Revolution period compounded the problem, resulting as it did in an overwhelming self-confidence on the part of all components of British society, including the church, whose members believed it was their duty to share the fruits of their good fortune with the uncivilized world. Thus a missionary hymn could pose the question:

> Shall we whose souls are lighted
> With wisdom from on high,
> Shall we to men benighted
> The lamp of life deny?[103]

The not so hidden agenda of the missionary, however, was that in exchange for bestowing the gift of civilization, the missionary hoped, on behalf of the Empire, to extract from those new colonies the raw materials needed to augment the success of the Industrial Revolution. Anthony Grant, in the 1843 Bampton Lecture to the University of Oxford, gleefully recognized that the Empire through her colonies was "brought into contact with almost the entire heathen world" thereby laying on the church a "national responsibility . . . to discern God's Hand in this conjecture and to execute His will."[104] One future missionary who read his work and who "shared his sense of providential alliance between empire and mission" was Robert Gray, first bishop of Cape Town.[105]

The struggle for racial justice on the part of the South African church, therefore, is more like a history of fits and starts, or as Bishop Nuttall describes it, "like a vein of gold in the quartz, shining in different ways."[106] It is the story of individuals and groups of individuals who were courageous enough to challenge prevailing attitudes. Thankfully, owing in no small measure to the Anglo-Catholic influence on the life of the church, such personages were not in short supply in the CPSA. As early as 1877, N. J. Merriman, bishop of Grahamstown, called on the prime minister of the Cape. He lodged a complaint that, following the frontier wars, land had been taken from the Ngqika tribe, among whom the Anglican Church had begun a mission, and had given it to white farmers.

Although his entreaty fell on deaf ears, it was a significant step, since the idea that the European government and the Anglican Church were identified as a single bloc was thus challenged. Merriman's protest can be seen as an early example of the influx of liberal thought which helped to shape church policy, and which began to take root in the latter part of the nineteenth century. Such liberalism was characterized by a "belief in the importance and dignity of the individual without regard to color or culture, . . . and the conviction that society can achieve political stability, economic prosperity and social justice by human effort and at an evolutionary pace."[107] It was an evolutionary process to be sure, and such views were by no means universally held. But there were identifiable signs of hope.

In the same year that Merriman made his futile trip to Cape Town, the province, under the leadership of William West Jones, Gray's successor, in an effort to coordinate missionary work, sponsored the first of several provincial missionary conferences. During one of these gatherings, a committee recommended that "the time had come for African Christians to take a fuller share in the legislative assemblies of the church." Subsequent meetings addressed weightier matters. The 1918 Conference passed a resolution that it was "incumbent upon the white races to see to it that the native races of South Africa shall not be exploited for the benefit of the white races, nor forced into a position of servitude, but may have space in this country an opportunity for development . . . to become useful and industrious citizens." A bolder resolution was passed in 1923, urging the government to the "need of a careful revision of the Pass Laws . . . so as to avoid the frequent arrest of Natives."[108]

The Question of Indigenous Leadership

While such provincial actions were being taken, progress inched along at the diocesan level. In 1907, William Carter, bishop of Pretoria, another in the long line of Tractarian prelates who would succeed Jones as archbishop, joined with leaders of other denominations in "a classical statement of the case for basing political rights on other grounds than race or color." He also signed a petition to the British Parliament to intervene to prevent the imposition of a color bar. When the matter reached the House of Lords, however, Randall Davidson, Archbishop of Canterbury, in a comment reflective of the sentiment of the period, "regretted its inclusion, and specifically likened Africans to children who must be brought to a maturer and more responsible state."[109] During his episcopate, Carter, believing in indigenous ministries, ordained the first twelve African priests in the province, thus challenging the prevailing view that missionary work was the work of white priests and native evangelists. Later, as archbishop, he wrote to the South African government protesting the restrictions that had been placed on the black populace.

Two important factors undermined the church's effectiveness in the area of race relations. The first is that there was often no follow-through. Synods, commissions and committees often lacked or were unwilling to wield the power necessary to achieve concrete results. The other impediment was more serious, that the church found itself in the position of asking society to remove a mote from its eye while the church still had a beam in its own. The South African church, while demanding that Africans be accorded their rightful place in South African society, were opposed to black representation in diocesan synods. Although standing in opposition to a color bar which restricted Africans to separate facilities and segregated housing, the church unabashedly maintained separate congregations for whites and "natives." While advocating for the African to take leadership roles in society, the church effectively prevented the election of black priests as bishops.

The matter of a "native episcopate" was a perennial one in provincial synods and other church bodies, which in their deliberations were often less than enthusiastic about the idea. In 1938, for example, the Provincial Missionary Conference passed a resolution that Africans might be appointed as *assistant* bishops "when suitable men are available and when such appointments would help forward the work of the Church." Although delegates to Synod always made it clear that there was no obstacle to the election of an African bishop, their specification that blacks be appointed as assistant bishops made it clear that they did not envisage the possibility of a black diocesan presiding over a diocese in which white clergy were in the majority.

In the early 1940s, Hazael Maimane and James Calata, African priests of Pretoria and Grahamstown, respectively, were forthright in laying a charge of racism at the door of the South African church. Calling attention to the racial segregation practiced by the church, they advocated for the creation of a separate African branch of the church, as a parallel jurisdiction within the Anglican Communion. Remarkably, the bishops of the province, who were quite willing to countenance a *de facto* separation of the races, opined that the proposal of parallel churches, which would be tantamount to a *de jure* separation, was schismatic, and therefore "contrary to Catholic Custom and Order."[110]

At the time such issues were not peculiar to the South African church. The question of clerical leadership was always a thorny one in places where the very success of the missionary enterprise resulted in the burgeoning of the "native" population and the natural consequence that leaders should emerge from its ranks. In 1864, for example, when Samuel Ajayi Crowther was consecrated for Nigeria, his letters patent were so worded as to ensure he would only have jurisdiction over the rural native population. He was to minister "to the countries of West Africa beyond the Queen's domains," specifically excluding British colonies where he would be in the anomalous position of being in authority over white Englishmen.[111] In the Episcopal Church, USA, there was vociferous objection to blacks in the episcopate, a matter that was temporarily resolved through the consecration of two "suffragan bishops for colored work."[112]

As we examine the way the church carried out its mission between the mid-nineteenth and mid-twentieth centuries, it is easy for us to accuse the church of racist behavior. We find incongruous the statement that "the church succumbed to the ideology of segregation, and in practice supported the maintenance of white power, although adhering to the ideal of non-racial justice."[113] But the reason that such a statement can stand is that the church believed that as long as missionaries provided for the spiritual needs of those to whom they brought the Gospel, they had done their job.[114] The church embraced a theology of mission which reflected rather than challenged the dominant themes of imperialism, capitalism, and colonialism. The idea that races (or classes) should mix, therefore, was simply not part of the world view of English missionaries.[115] The words of Cecil Frances Alexander were still an apt description of the church's missiology:

The rich man in his castle, the poor man at his gate,
God made them high and lowly, and ordered his estate.[116]

The Church Finds Her Voice

It is ironic that it was not until the South African government demanded that churches be segregated that the church was finally persuaded to believe that the separation of the races was morally wrong. "As the nation goes, so goes the church."[117] If the church seemed to condone the government's racist policies, it was because of what might be described as an identity crisis on the church's part. The church's hierarchy did not become anti-apartheid activists until they made the transition from being reactive, that is, objecting (often mildly and ineffectually) to the laws which made second-class citizens of black South Africans, to being proactive, that it, taking a prophetic stand, declaring government policies to be immoral, and then taking specific actions to redress the failures of the society and the church in which they found themselves. It should be made clear, however, that a change in position at the church's top echelons came about gradually, first because many church leaders, through their prophetic witness, challenged the church's officialdom to take action.

As early as 1944, for example, Michael Scott founded the Campaign for Rights and Justice, whose purpose was to obtain full and direct political representation for all and to abolish all discriminatory legislation. He received no support from the church hierarchy, whose "emphasis was on moderation, on obedience to law and on attempts to create racial good will, albeit in an increasingly narrow arena."[118] Although activists at the time, both black and white, were also committed to racial harmony, they "did not adopt the tendency of the bishops to separate the search for political and social rights for blacks from the missionary activity of the church."[119] Such prophetic voices found it increasingly frustrating that the bishops of the CPSA, for example, could issue a statement condemning racial discrimination as "morally wrong," while at the same time defending its own discriminatory practices, for example, in the administration of its church schools.[120]

The other, more influential factor which had some bearing on the church's change in attitude was external. As the government's policies became increasingly and overtly racist, the church hierarchy found it more and more difficult to attempt to defend, rationalize, condone or ignore such actions.

Owing, for example, to the policies implemented by the first Afrikaner-dominated government in 1948, "the churches turned more and more to formal protest," and as "new legislation . . . intensified racist regulations . . . it was not long before events pushed formal protest into channels of passive resistance."[121] DeGruchy concurs, and suggests that the church's newfound position emerged from a sense of penance. "In spite of failures in their own fellowship, the English-speaking churches spoke out strongly against what was happening at virtually every step along the apartheid route during the first decade of the National Party rule." He also points out that the government's actions were so egregious that even the Dutch Reformed Church joined in the protest.[122]

Protest, it has been observed, is not the same as resistance, so it is not surprising that the church proved less than effective in its fight against apartheid until such time as it adopted a clearly prophetic and proactive role. Until it did, its voice was just another among the many groups who were taking the government to task, and their actions in this regard gave credence to the allegation that the church was mixing religion and politics. One South African ecumenist sees the value, even the necessity, of such actions when they "address relevantly the critical socio-political and ethical issues of our society," but maintains that such protest must be done in such a way "that it sets the church apart from the party-political debate."[123] In other words, it is not enough for the church merely to chime in with other groups; it must bring to the table theological arguments clearly rooted in the Gospel. When the church upholds such ideals, it ceases to be just another facet of society, and becomes, instead, to use Gore's words, "the home of the best moral conscience of the community."[124]

This progression from reactive to proactive, from apathetic to prophetic, is related to another phenomenon, and that is the Africanization or indigenization of the church. If it is true, as Luke Pato contends, that the biblical message must be proclaimed "in such a manner that Jesus is not only understood, but also seen to be a Saviour of Africa, providing answers to the questions of the Africans,"[125] then it follows that the message of liberation will take on an enhanced authenticity when its messengers are those who themselves have been denied basic human rights. Anglicanism in South Africa was first seen as the religious arm of the Crown, responsible for doing its part in the enterprise of Empire-building. Well into the twentieth century, it was "almost a state church [with] close political, economic and social connections between the Church and authorities."[126]

The church later entered a period of advocacy, during which the vision of many English missionaries (and later some white South Africans) "extended beyond the Church's functional dependency upon the dominant political system."[127] During this period, missionaries began to see themselves less as doing the Crown's bidding, and more as advocating for the rights of the people. Such activity was the fruit of a social Gospel, yet "the maintenance of white power and the exercise of social control were significant constituents of liberal policy and was reflected in the work of the church."[128] Most recently, indigenous leaders in the South African church have helped to bring about "changed hearts and renewed minds [needed] to break the shackles of the Church's increasingly-evident complicity in oppression and injustice, in order to ensure that the flickering flame of the resurrection burns brightly on this sub-continent of Africa."[129]

The South African Church Cautiously Confronts Apartheid

During the time that these issues were widely debated, Geoffrey Hare Clayton occupied, successively, the two most visible bishoprics in the Church of South Africa. He was bishop of Johannesburg from 1934 until 1948, when he was elected Archbishop of Cape Town, a position he held for eight years until his death. He was, like Gray, the son of a bishop, and like most of the bishops and priests of the province, a staunch Anglo-Catholic churchman. His biographer writes: "According to von Hugel there were three elements of religion, the catholic-sacramental-social, the liberal-rational-intellectual, and the evangelical-biblical-mystical. . . . Clayton maintained all three to the full."[130]

But it was in his characterization as liberal-rational-intellectual that Clayton exemplified the spirit of his generation. The CPSA in the mid-twentieth century "demonstrated the weaknesses and strengths of South African liberalism." While the church made (often successful) attempts to mitigate the social and economic hardships of black South Africans, and often encouraged their self-expression, it nevertheless operated within a system that recognized segregation and white control as normative.[131] It was not until the very end of his life and ministry that Clayton could extricate himself from those tenets which had been inculcated in him as both an English gentleman and a missionary.

When Geoffrey Clayton became bishop of Johannesburg, the word "apartheid" was not in the dictionary, yet it existed in every way but name. It was in 1948, however, the year of Clayton's translation to Cape Town, that the government began to enact laws to put the various aspects of apartheid into effect, prohibiting, for example, marriage and sexual relations across racial lines, and making it impossible for non-whites to vote.[132]

Much like slavery in the United States, apartheid was predicated on economic interests. A complex system built upon this economic foundation, and predicated on an intricately designed pecking order, apartheid had at its core four major tenets. First, South Africa would be comprised of four racial groups—White, Coloured, Indian and African. Second, whites, deemed to be the civilized race, were entrusted with absolute control over the state. Third, white interests were determined to prevail over black interests, the state not being obliged to provide equal facilities for the subordinate races. Finally, the white racial group formed a single nation (with Afrikaans- and English-speaking components) while Africans belonged to distinct nations or potential nations, a formula designed to ensure that the white nation would be the largest in the country.[133]

Clearly, it was the enforcement of the last of these features of apartheid which was the most insidious. A series of laws was passed to ensure that Africans, who comprised seventy percent of the population, would be denied access to power. The African population was grouped into eight (later ten) territories, also called "reserves" or "homelands." Each homeland theoretically had the potential of becoming an independent "nation," albeit administered under white tutelage by a set of Bantu authorities, who were for the most part hereditary chiefs. The government, disingenuously, likened this provision for "independence" to the practice of decolonization of European holdings elsewhere in Africa.

The homeland system achieved for the South African government what it set out to do. The reserves were seen "as the national home of the black population from which they migrate as necessary to European areas *to perform what tasks are dictated by the latter's needs.*"[134] Moreover, through this system, blacks, nearly three-quarters of the population, owned but thirteen percent of the land. As apartheid flourished with the homeland system at full throttle, the

African population was virtually bereft of any political or economic power. The average per capita income of black South Africans was about ten percent of whites'. Most significantly, to ensure control and the implementation of every aspect of this nefarious system, South Africa was governed entirely by the all-white Parliament in Cape Town, a system which prevented other racial groups from having a say in the nation's administration.

It is worth noting that in the apartheid system, education was mandatory for whites, but not for blacks. In fact, were it not for the churches, including the CPSA, who historically believed that "the best way to Christianize and civilize the Africans was to provide them with a European type of academic education,"[135] there would have been virtually no native education. Indeed, Ndungane points out that the church presented a clear threat to the government. One of the major reasons for the attacks by the apartheid government against the churches was because of the caliber of education which the churches provided. Since the government's approach to Bantu education was to maintain an inferior system which it hoped would discourage Natives from high achievement, it routinely closed church schools which consistently produced leaders in every sphere of South African society.[136] It is clear that such an intrusion into the church's life and mission would have resulted in moving the church away from a reactive and toward a more proactive stance. The church, instead of voicing objection to the government's educational policies, had created instead a parallel educational system which was often superior to the state-run schools. Through such a tactic, the church could "quietly" raise up leaders. The state's new policy made such an approach impossible, and the church was forced to object to it more openly.

The church that Clayton had been called to lead was but a reflection of the society of which it was a part. Black clergy, who were assigned only to black congregations, received a salary of about one-third of that of their white counterparts. No blacks had any leadership positions in the councils of the church. Clayton's style was a cautious one; he was not a boat-rocker, and therefore did not take any overt steps to redress these anomalies. Like his fellow bishops of the province, his "emphasis was on moderation, on obedience to law and on attempts to create racial good will, albeit in an increasingly narrow arena."[137] Indeed, he believed for a long time that the church should be, strictly speaking, neutral; the church best serves society when it is being itself, that is, focusing its primary attention on the salvation of the individual.

The church, he said, must take its stand "between the two fires of worldliness and unworldliness."[138]

Nevertheless, in his episcopal charges delivered at diocesan synods in Johannesburg, Clayton decried such injustices as the disproportionate taxes paid by Africans, the government's penchant for sending Africans to jail for trivial offenses, and the paucity of educational opportunities for natives. But even in his gradualism, he was unequivocal in his views about the role of the Christian. In one of his charges, he said: "A Christian must regard himself as God's subject even before he is the subject of the government of his country. God is not identified with the state . . . God is revealed through Jesus Christ, and a Christian must judge the actions of the state in the light of his knowledge of God through Jesus Christ."[139]

An Odious Word is Born

By 1948, the word "apartheid," the Afrikaans word for "apartness," was indeed in the South African's dictionary. It can be said that it was in that year that racism came of age in South Africa. Although racial discrimination had long been entrenched in South African society and was enforced through its Constitution, the government-endorsed policy of apartheid changed the meaning of racism for South Africans, "differing in degree and direction, rather than in kind, from the policies which had gone before."[140] It was a policy designed to maintain and protect the white race as a distinctive group. The white race, under this system, would be placed in a position of guardianship and trusteeship, while each racial group would, theoretically, develop "within its own national boundary." The detribalized Bantu would remain attached to their "homelands," ten supposedly independent nations, and would be "visitors" in white South Africa where they would not be eligible to share in the political and social rights enjoyed by whites. One historian has made it clear what apartheid did *not* mean: "It did not mean equality; it did not mean race mixing; it did not mean integration and the extension of rights to the non-white. [Apartheid] was synonymous with white racial supremacy."[141]

It was clear that a new day had dawned for South Africa, and for lovers of justice and equality the portents were ominous to say the least. As John DeGruchy observes, "there was no doubt . . . that the English-speaking churches and other denominations belonging to the Christian Council realized that a new political phenomenon had entered the scene, and that it contradicted the hopes which they had for the future of the churches and the country."[142] The problem was exacerbated by the fact that the new system purported to be based on the Christian principle of right and justice. It is noteworthy that 1948 was the year of the Lambeth Conference at which the bishops in attendance decried racism as inconsistent with the Gospel. Emboldened by the example of the world's bishops, the bishops of the Province of Central Africa, at Clayton's encouragement, issued a statement later that year in which they said that only through harmonious relationships between various racial groups could South Africa hope to be reconciled. "If, on the other hand, Europeans seek to preserve to themselves the exclusive benefits of Western Civilization, and to allow the non-Europeans merely its burdens, South Africans will inexorably draw apart into mutually antagonistic racial groups."

South Africa's bishops may not have been aware of how prophetic a statement this was, and moreover, how it presaged the transition they were to make from a reactive to a proactive stance. To express the wish that the races be reconciled was nothing new; they had often voiced such a concern, in synodical resolutions, in episcopal charges and even in letters to government officials. What made this statement noteworthy was the allusion to the *means* by which reconciliation was to take place, namely the necessity for whites to concede some of the benefits and privileges that had so long inhered to them solely because of the color of their skin.

Geoffrey Clayton and Trevor Huddleston Lock Horns

Given the escalated stakes, Clayton's measured and irenic approach in the face of this new reality was rejected by many of the clergy and people of the CPSA, who frankly believed that his approach was unequal to the task at hand. If apartheid was to be effectively challenged, a more forceful tactic was called for. Those within the church who were impatient with the archbishop comprised a "loyal opposition" who proved to be a thorn in Clayton's flesh. In this internecine battle, the archbishop's chief antagonist was Trevor Huddleston, a priest of the Community of the Resurrection who was attached to the parish of Christ the King in the township of Sophiatown. The major differences between the Claytonians and the Huddlestonians was one of methodology. For when all was said and done, both groups agreed that racism was incompatible with the Christian gospel; both would hold that the church has the right, indeed the duty, to make the political status quo subject to the imperatives of the Gospel. The points of digression centered around the issues of if, when, how, and under what circumstances the church should act.

There was a good reason that Huddleston and the people in his camp, such as Bishop Ambrose Reeves, Patrick Duncan, and Michael Scott, did not agree with Clayton and his ideologues on how the church should oppose apartheid. Huddleston and his friends had worked closely with blacks, fighting against apartheid in the political arena. Ambrose Reeves, who had been trained by the Mirfield Fathers, succeeded Clayton as bishop of Johannesburg. He "abhorred apartheid, and everything directly or indirectly connected with it. He regarded it, and the treatment of non-whites in the name of apartheid, as unjust and unchristian. He believed that the Church had a duty to speak out against the system, the philosophy which underlay it, and the actions it provoked."[143] Michael Scott, an Englishman, had returned to South Africa from a stint in India to serve as assistant priest at a black mission, St. Alban's, Johannesburg and as chaplain to an orphanage for colored children in Sophiatown. He had previously worked at a mission to lepers in the Cape.[144] Patrick Duncan, a layman, had been a district officer with the British Colonial Service in Basotholand, where he was very close to black political opinion. He became a prominent figure in anti-government demonstrations. Clayton, by contrast, could claim no such experience. Huddleston's group maintained that the Claytonians' strategy grew out of a theology of paternalism, developed at an arm's length from the problem, and not based on identification with those at the grassroots level.

While it would be unfair to describe Huddleston as the most radical of the group, it is true that his fame, which came in no small measure from his book, *Naught for Your Comfort,* set him apart from his colleagues. Too, his charisma and his confrontational and persuasive activism gave him a wider audience. A few characteristics distinguished his teaching from that of the church establishment. First, he made it clear that he identified *with* poor blacks, and was not merely doing good works on their behalf. In a letter to the editor of a local newspaper he wrote: "In South Africa the whip now falls on black shoulders, not on white. And in my opinion the only possible choice for Christians is *identification* with the African people: a sharing in their suffering as far as is possible—and a determination to do all in one's power to make known what is unjust and to strive against it."[145] It can be said here that Father Huddleston changed the theology of mission by substituting one preposition for another. Typically, missionaries, evangelical and catholic, spoke of working *among* groups, a phrase which always creates a distance between missionary and missionized. Huddleston's approach, identification *with* the Africans, connotes instead a solidarity.

Second, Huddleston, whom Tutu has described as "unrelenting in his fight against apartheid,"[146] was among the first to declare that the racial problems in South Africa were not just local, but global, and so he could, without apology, enlist the world's assistance. "It seems to me," he wrote in *Naught for Your Comfort*, "that the only way to meet this thing as a Christian is to try at least to arouse the Christian conscience throughout the world." In a suggestion that proved prophetic, he even urged, in 1953, a cultural boycott of South Africa, an idea which unleashed the wrath of the South African synod of bishops. The bishops argued that such a tactic was unfair since it compromised "such expressions of the Christian conscience of the influence which they might otherwise exercise."[147] In making the radical suggestion of a boycott, Huddleston was saying that because of the egregiousness of South Africa's racial policies, that nation should be prevented from profiting from the performances of the world's artists and musicians. The other side of this coin was that he asked the artists if they could in all conscience perform before all-white audiences. A similar philosophy would be applied some three decades later when the world participated in imposing economic sanctions on South Africa.

Lastly, the monk from Mirfield was not afraid to name the church as complicit in the problem. Far from a Claytonian neutrality, Huddleston's theology could not brook the idea of an indifferent church. According to Father George Guiver, CR, present Superior of the Order, "few things grieved Trevor more than the failure of church members to act. And to those who accused the church of being political, he simply asked them to read Jeremiah, Amos and Isaiah as proof that God has always been very much concerned about the way society was organized."[148] In a now famous letter to *The Observer* on 10 October 1954, in response to the church's silence on the banning of Oliver Tambo for his activities in the African National Congress, Father Huddleston excoriated his fellow Christians:

The Church sleeps on. It sleeps on while 60,000 people are moved from their homes in the interest of a fantastic racial theory; . . . it sleeps on while a dictatorship is swiftly being created over all Native Affairs in the Union, so that speech and movement and association are no longer free. The Church sleeps on—though it occasionally talks in its sleep and expects (or does it?) the Government to listen. The day is drawing near when the African Christian would accept no longer the authority of the sleeping Church and he will cast it off.

Huddleston Whisked from South Africa

In 1956, Father Raymond Raynes, the Superior of the Community of the Resurrection, recalled Trevor Huddleston to the mother house at Mirfield, announcing that Huddleston would assume the post of Guardian of the Novices. There has been widespread speculation as to the reason for his removal, but it is widely believed that given Father Trevor's outspokenness, which had riled both church and state, his life might well have been in danger. By the time Huddleston took leave of his beloved South Africa, there was clearly a tension between him and the church establishment, even causing some to believe that Clayton had had a hand in the recall. While it has never been established that Clayton was responsible for Huddleston's removal, it is a matter of record that "Clayton made it clear that he did not want Huddleston back."[149] At one point, Clayton had even resigned as Visitor to the Community. Developments soon after his departure made it clear that Trevor Huddleston had left his mark on the CPSA. Archbishop Tutu said of his mentor: "Trevor Huddleston was passionate in his commitment to justice and spoke out fearlessly to oppose the awfulness of apartheid. . . . He was deeply prayerful and we learned by example more than precept that the spiritual was utterly crucial and indispensable for an authentic Christian life."[150]

The formation of that spiritual life did not begin in the cloisters at Mirfield, and was not limited, as was the case of many Anglo-Catholic religious, to outward and visible signs of worship and expressions of piety and devotion. His spiritual development and social consciousness were two sides of the same coin. An obituary cites the experiences of his seeing barefoot, undernourished children at a mission run by his school in Camberwell;

watching an Indian boy being turned away from the door of his college at Oxford; seeing hunger marchers protesting in the streets of that university town; and ministering to his working class parishioners at his first curacy, St. Mark's Swindon.[151] When he visited the Community of the Resurrection prior to entering it as a postulant in 1939, he commented that he "was much impressed . . . [by] the way the brethren were very aware of the world. It was not a reclusive community; it was an active missionary order."[152]

When he was posted to Sophiatown, therefore, Father Huddleston had no difficulty in understanding social activism as an integral part of pastoral care. Where some clergy might have, in a patronizing way, prayed for or with a parishioner who faced a serious problem which resulted in deprivation of adequate housing or sufficient food or mistreatment in the workplace, Huddleston became an advocate, appearing, in his Benedictine habit, in the police station, the judge's chamber, the courtroom or the employer's office, unabashedly confronting the authority responsible for the situation. At his side was the hapless parishioner arrested for being found without his pass, or who had been savagely beaten during his detainment. And when Huddleston was rebuffed by such an authority, he sought another solution, such as when he inaugurated the African Children's Feeding Scheme upon learning that only white children were entitled to a midday meal at school. He brought the same sense of dedication to a cause when thrown into a wider arena in which he could plead the case for an entire class of people, and not just an individual or family.

When he did so, his actions were invariably covered in the press, and when they were not, he not infrequently issued press releases, or sent copies of his sermons and other public pronouncements to the Johannesburg newspapers. Even some of his supporters accused him of being "too fond of personal publicity and acclaim, too keen to see his picture in the papers."[153] But I think such allegations were unfounded. Huddleston, who took seriously his vows of poverty, chastity and obedience. sought no glory. Rather, he intuitively understood what many turn-the-other-cheek Christians do not—that one of the keys to effecting social change is raising the consciousness of the public around a given issue. The local and international publicity that Huddleston received made the world aware of the injustices of apartheid, and began to plant the seeds of indignation in the minds of people around the globe. Such seeds were a significant factor in the eventual dismantling of apartheid. Given that that dismantling would not have happened as soon as it did, or in the way that it did, were it not for the pressure exerted by an indignant global community, it is clear that Huddleston's instincts were well founded.

When all was said and done, Trevor Huddleston was convinced that apartheid was irredeemably evil, and "he believed it was right and necessary to defy unjust laws and oppose the arbitrary, racialist use of authority."[154] For this reason, he was as quick to attack gradualism as a method of confronting apartheid as he was in condemning apartheid itself. This basic difference in approach accounted for the palpable tension between the humble monk from Mirfield and His Grace the Archbishop of Cape Town.

Father Huddleston was effective as a priest and anti-apartheid activist because he was not afraid to attack the root cause of the problem at hand. When I visited Sophiatown in August of 2004 for the inaugural "Naught for Your Comfort" lecture, I learned that when the Nationalist government came into power in 1948, it set about almost immediately to destroy Sophiatown. Desmond Tutu explains that the reason for that strategy was that Sophiatown "was an anomaly in their policy which regarded all black people as birds of passage, temporary denizens of the white man's town. Sophiatown stuck out as a sore thumb because, there, blacks had what was unacceptable, freehold title to their land."[155] It was Huddleston, according to Tutu, who helped to galvanize the people in their efforts to resist this. It proved to be a Sisyphean task, since the government succeeded in displacing black residents and presumptuously renaming the town Triomf. But Huddleston's determination was doubtless an inspiration to the people when, after Independence, they reclaimed the town, its name, and their beloved Church of Christ the King.

The South African Church Vigorously Confronts Apartheid

Huddleston's spirit even had an effect, if a residual one, on his nemesis Archbishop Clayton. In 1957, the South African government introduced legislation in the form of the Native Laws Amendment Bill, which sought to exert control over any institution, including the church, which admitted even an individual black person. In its infamous "church clause," the bill made it obligatory for church buildings to be segregated, and further decreed that it would be an offense to admit blacks into white churches. Confronted with and affronted by the passing of this law (which was never abolished but was seldom enforced), Clayton's ideology metamorphosed from gradualism into a kind of Huddlestonian activism. The government's action made him realize that the style of liberalism he had for so long espoused had ceased to be effective, and as a result he "committed the church to a new kind of struggle and a new understanding of mission."[156]

Clayton must have understood as he protested the government's actions that his new understanding of mission was one that had been long advocated by Trevor Huddleston. Such an understanding of the church's mission, the archbishop realized, might mean both breaking of the law and encouraging others to do so. Such an understanding meant being proactive instead of reactive. This was a frightening prospect for the law-abiding bishop who for so long had worked "within the system," a fear surpassed only by the repulsive prospect of incarceration. But the proposed new law was intolerable, and had to be challenged. Accordingly, he summoned to a meeting of the Emergency Committee of the Episcopal Synod the bishops of Grahamstown, Johannesburg, Pretoria and Natal. The committee's meeting on Shrove Tuesday and Ash Wednesday had as its sole agenda charting the church's course of action in light of the legislation, and weighing the consequences of any acts of civil disobedience which they might consider. Should the CPSA refuse to obey such a law? Should a public statement be issued? What course of action should be taken if the archbishop and/or other bishops were arrested for inciting people to disobey the law?

In the week preceding the meeting, Archbishop Clayton had drafted a letter to the Prime Minister. When his colleagues arrived at Bishopscourt, they perused the letter, and after making a few emendations, approved it. The final document stated that the church refused to recognize the right of the government to determine whom a minister of the Gospel could admit to public worship. Further, it reminded the government that the Constitution of the province provides for the participation of clergy and laity without regard to race. While acknowledging their duty to obey civil authority, the bishops also pointed out that they are under a higher authority. They concluded by stating, therefore, that if the bill were to become law, they would be able neither to obey it nor to counsel their clergy and people to obey it.[157]

The bishops' letter represented a significant shift in the CPSA's approach to racial issues. Verbal protests and gentle suggestions gave way, in this document, to an actual challenge and, even more significantly, to the threat of disobedience. The letter was to be Clayton's last official archiepiscopal act. He suffered a fatal heart attack on the very day he put his signature to it. The archbishop's physician listed the cause of death as "heart seizure," but many of his close associates, according to Clayton's biographer, believed that "his decision to defy the powers that be had played a great part in this sudden death."[158]

The Anglican bishops' actions (and Clayton's death) served to motivate other churches. The Roman Catholic bishops issued a statement that their churches "must and shall remain open to all without regard to their racial origin." An ecumenical body, the Christian Council of South Africa, declared, "We shall be forced to disregard the law." The Methodist Church, in a telegram to the Prime Minister, expressed a similar sentiment.[159] In the wake of the South African government's unprecedented attempt to use the law to interfere in the affairs of the churches, and of the churches' reaction to it, it became clear that a new era in church-state relations had begun.

South African Injustice on a World Stage

There was no obvious successor to Clayton, and for this reason, and because they could not imagine anyone else at the church's helm who could lead the fight against apartheid, the provincial synod of bishops had refused to accept Clayton's resignation, which he submitted in October 1956 to take effect the following Easter. His sudden death (which came, as it turned out, a month and a half before his intended retirement date) threw them into a quandary. After several rounds of fruitless balloting, Joost deBlank's name was introduced. He was at the time bishop of Stepney (a suffragan see of London).[160] His being Dutch-born led some to believe that he might be good for relations with the Reformed Church. He was, like virtually all of his predecessors, a unwavering Anglo-Catholic. His early pronouncements made it clear that he was picking up where Clayton had left off. His first charge to the diocese, in December 1958, sounded a familiar theological chord:

> One thing has surprised me, and that is the vociferous minority who believe that a concern for humanity and social justice is politics and not Christianity. Such thinking reflected a lopsided view of the incarnation. God became man in Christ Jesus, and so all life, including its political aspect, was the sphere of Christian obedience.

Mindful, perhaps, of Huddleston's indictment of the church, deBlank took steps to ensure that the province was not guilty of the sin of apartheid. But deBlank's style was not merely to issue platitudinous statements. Catholic churchman that he was, he believed in outward and visible signs. Under him, the diocese established a mixed (white and colored) school. During his watch, black and colored clergy celebrated the Eucharist in the Cathedral in Cape Town. He worked against apartheid with a women's organization called the Black Sash. Early in his primacy the archbishop preached in Holy Trinity Cathedral in Accra, Ghana, and made a statement whose theology would become the core of Desmond Tutu's theology three decades later. "The conflict between the Church and state in South Africa," he declared, "is at heart not a political one but a religious one, based not on political theory but on theological principle." These words provoked the South African Prime Minister, who launched a verbal attack on the archbishop, questioning his right to "besmirch" his adopted country abroad. DeBlank's famous reply was an offer to the Prime Minister: "For the sake of South Africa I am prepared to withdraw from the country as Archbishop and Metropolitan if Dr. Verwoerd will withdraw as Prime Minister and return to his native land. His native land, it may be recalled, is the same as mine."[161]

The Sharpeville Massacre in 1960 was to deBlank's archiepiscopate what the Native Laws Amendment Bill was to Clayton's. But whereas Clayton changed tactics on account of the government's action, deBlank pursued similar tactics, but shifted into high gear. Firing from armored cars known as "caspars," the police killed sixty-seven innocent and unarmed African demonstrators. This, coupled with the wanton burning of churches, made it blatantly clear how serious the situation had become. So far as the government was concerned, deBlank's most inflammatory act was his condemnation of the Dutch Reformed Church, the sole Christian body in South Africa that had not issued a statement condemning government actions at Sharpeville. He dispatched an emissary to Geneva to the headquarters of the World Council of Churches to inform that body that the continuing support for apartheid by the Dutch Reformed Churches "makes African hostility to the Christian Faith inevitable. The future of Christianity in this country," continued the archbishop, "demands our complete dissociation from the Dutch Reformed Church attitude."[162] An article in *Time* reported the archbishop's actions, keeping the world abreast of the harsh reality of racial oppression in South Africa.

Later, the bishops of the CPSA demanded that the DRC be expelled from the WCC. Although the WCC did not comply with that demand, the involvement of the WCC and the whole Anglican Communion (whose members deBlank had asked to participate in a day of prayer for Sharpeville) were yet additional steps taken by Archbishop deBlank in bringing the world's attention not only to the political, but the theological and spiritual challenges of apartheid. Nineteen-sixty was also the year that Prime Minister Harold Macmillan visited South Africa. In his speech to the Parliament in Pretoria, he avowed, "We reject the idea of any inherent superiority of one race over another." Then he added prophetically that in fifty years these particular differences would be regarded as of historical interest only! The British Prime Minister's words lent support to the archbishop's utterances during a year (in many ways his *annus horribilis*) in which he emerged as an uncompromising church leader. Building on the foundations of his predecessors, he had become the "scourge of apartheid."

Passing on the Baton

DeBlank's successors in office continued to build on the foundation of his prophetic ministry. Robert Selby Taylor, successively bishop of Northern Rhodesia, Pretoria and Grahamstown before becoming archbishop, was in temperament more like Clayton than deBlank. Reserved and methodical, he proved to be quietly effective. Early in his primacy, in 1966, he called a meeting which eventually led to the foundation of the University Christian Movement. It was an organization of black students which became a vehicle for black consciousness, although it was criticized for being under the control of whites.[163]

At a national conference of the South African Council of Churches in 1971, Taylor observed that the time had passed when it was enough for the South African Council of Churches to pass resolutions condemning racial prejudice and social injustice. He went on to state, "We must take positive action which will make it abundantly clear that we are not prepared to accept inequalities based on race." Bishop Ambrose Reeves observes, however, that "this was indeed a strong call for action but the Archbishop did not specify what action ought to be taken." Reeves also raised the question of whether Archbishop Taylor and others would not "resist any erosion of their present privileged position" if equality was achieved and blacks came into power.[164] Taylor's less than forceful approach can also be seen in his comments about civil disobedience. While accepting that there were instances "when the laws of the State become so onerous that a Christian is compelled to obey the voice of God expressed through his own conscience," he nevertheless allowed that it was "the State's duty to ensure the laws are kept, and [to] punish those who break the laws" regardless of what their motives might be.[165]

It was Taylor who encouraged Bill Burnett, Bishop of Pretoria, to take the position of General Secretary of the South African Council of Churches. Burnett was the first native-born South African to be elected bishop. In style, methodology and theology he was a polar opposite to Taylor, whom he succeeded as archbishop. Not long before his enthronement in St. George's Cathedral in 1974, the SACC had passed, with Bishop Burnett's enthusiastic endorsement, a resolution on conscientious objection. It was on its face an inflammatory document. Its preamble stated that the Republic of South Africa "is at present a fundamentally unjust and discriminatory society," and that its military forces "are being prepared to defend this unjust and discriminatory society."[166] Burnett, who enjoyed a reputation as one deeply committed both to charismatic renewal and liberation theology, preached a sermon at his enthronement in which he "called for a new Pentecost" and expressed the hope that people would take to heart the essence of the resolution. In an apt description of Burnett's ministry, DeGruchy comments: "The connection between charismatic renewal and nonviolence had found a powerful advocate."[167] Burnett firmly believed that apartheid could never be removed from the fabric of South African life until white South Africans acknowledged their own guilt. In an open letter to Prime Minister Vorster in 1976, he wrote: "Unless White Christians in particular admit the wrongs they have done to Black people and take action to redress them, there can be no possibility of healing in the land."

By default or by design, the primacy of the South African church seems to alternate between liberal, outspoken incumbents and conservative, soft-spoken incumbents. In 1981, Bill Burnett the charismatic activist was succeeded by Philip Russell, who came to the post from the new diocese of Port Elizabeth. He was not, however, the choice of the elective assembly of the province. The two contenders for the archbishopric were Michael Nuttall of Natal and Desmond Tutu, then General Secretary of the SACC, neither of whom managed to secure the necessary two-thirds vote. The matter passed to the Synod of Bishops, who saw in Russell a kind of compromise candidate, who, it was thought, might calm the waters which had been roiled during Burnett's term of office. He was known as a good administrator, who would bring some order to the office after the somewhat erratic ministry of Burnett. Russell had also long enjoyed a reputation for his involvement in social affairs. It has been observed "in his own quiet way . . . he helped end apartheid . . . [He] did this work by quietly speaking out against apartheid and through a trickle down effect, influencing the Anglican Church in South Africa."[168]

The pendulum swung dramatically again in 1986, when Russell was succeeded by Desmond Mpilo Tutu, who became the first black archbishop of the CPSA. His decisive election was nothing less than a kairotic moment. In placing Tutu at the helm of the storm-tossed South African church, the electorate was not expressing a belief that there would be smooth sailing ahead; rather the people of the province believed that Desmond Tutu was uniquely qualified to chart the church's course through seas which were both turbulent and previously un-navigated. They saw in Tutu a bishop cast in the mold of Cyprian, the fourth-century bishop of Carthage in Northern Africa, who understood himself as a symbol of church unity, the *glutinum*, or glue which kept the church together.[169] They saw in him one who could bring black and white together, precisely because his theology prevented him from seeing liberation as a black man's problem, and his experience made it impossible for him to see blacks as the white man's burden: "We are engaged in the black liberation struggle," Tutu said, "because we are also deeply concerned for white liberation. . . . God wants . . . to set us free *for our service of one another* in a more just and open society in South Africa."[170]

They also saw in Desmond Tutu a bishop modeled after another African bishop, Augustine of Hippo, who said, *"Vobis enim sum episcopus, vobiscum sum Christianus"* ("For you I am your bishop but with you I am a Christian").[171] Tutu was one who was involved in and identified with the struggle for liberation in South Africa in a way that no other candidate for the position could claim. After being duly elected, Tutu was enthroned in St. George's Cathedral, and then took up residence in Bishopscourt, the official suburban residence of his predecessors. But because of the Group Areas Act, he was guilty of a criminal offense simply for living there, since blacks were not allowed to live in an area designated for white residents without first obtaining a special permit from the government. In his first act of defiance as archbishop, Tutu refused to apply for such a permit, but no charges were ever preferred against him. But the supreme irony lay in the fact that despite being in possession of all the trappings of archiepiscopal office, Desmond Mpilo Tutu, Nobel laureate and archbishop and metropolitan of the Church in the Province of Southern Africa, was nevertheless a South African citizen who did not have the right to vote. The archbishop as a symbol of the suffering servant was a palpable one.

With Tutu's election, South African Anglicanism had come of age. Henceforth, it could no longer be seen as a missionary church but an indigenous church. The Church in the Province of South Africa was now in the hands of those to whom Robert Gray had been dispatched to bring the Gospel a century and a half earlier.

Chapter V

Mixing Politics and Religion: The Prophetic Ministry of Desmond Mpilo Tutu

Tutu is a political priest in two ways. First, he resolved to work through the church to fight apartheid. Second, he sought to anchor the political struggle theologically. Thus, Tutu inspired the church in South Africa to dismantle apartheid in order to bring about a new model of how communities may negotiate with one another in a new South Africa. This commitment . . . put him at the center of a political storm.

—Michael Battle[172]

It's dangerous to put Archbishop Desmond and God together.

—Mother Vivian Harber, Assistant Priest,
St. George's Cathedral, Cape Town

Tutu's Theology: A Seamless Garment

About fifteen years ago, I attended a meeting of the All-Africa Conference of Churches in Lome, Togo, as an observer from the Episcopal Church. Desmond Tutu was there as president. In a question-and-answer session, someone asked the archbishop if, in his role in South Africa's struggle against apartheid, it was appropriate for him to mix politics and religion. With his trademark twinkle in his eyes and a broad smile, he told the assembled delegates that P. W. Botha had raised the same question, criticizing him for his social activism, and suggesting that he go back to his chapel and pray. The questioner in Lome got the same answer as the President of South Africa: "Anyone who thinks you shouldn't mix politics and religion has not been reading the same Bible I've been reading!"

The belief that politics and religion should exist in separate and distinct spheres has long been a popular tenet among certain religionists and politicians. They hold a conviction that there is an irreconcilable dichotomy between the sacred and the secular, the holy and the profane. The members of each group believe that by not trampling on the other's turf, they can play it safe and avoid offense. And this is probably the answer to the question Tutu himself poses: "Why does the cry 'Don't mix religion with politics' have such a long pedigree?"[173] When Tutu says that such persons have not been reading the same Bible that he has, he is making the statement that the Bible is a book—or more correctly, a collection of books, fraught with political intrigue. Moses the Liberator, who led an enslaved people out of bondage in Egypt, the prophets who castigated their people for being "at ease in Zion" while the poor begged for bread, and Jesus himself, who was crucified because he posed a threat both to established government and established religion were all caught in the vortex of the political reality of their day.

Any understanding of the life and work of Desmond Mpilo Tutu begins with grasping the fact that his "theology and spirituality are inseparable from his political life."[174] Everyone who has attempted to write about his life has seized on this basic truth, if in different ways. Du Boulay writes: "His desire for peace is matched by such indignation at the injustice of apartheid that his remarks . . . fuel flames of outrage. . . . He has shown, in both words and deeds, that religion and politics cannot be separated."[175] Indeed, the topic was the subject of a dissertation by M. Gideon Khabela, chaplain to the Truth and Reconciliation Commission, entitled *A Seamless Garment: Church and Politics in the Ministry of Desmond Tutu.*[176]

Desmond the Political Theologian, or, if you will, the Theological Politician, was a role which Archbishop Tutu had played on various stages throughout his life. It could be seen in the leadership he provided as dean of Johannesburg and subsequently as bishop of Lesotho. It could be seen in the period during which he was Secretary General of the South Africa Council of Churches. It was further developed in the brief period that he occupied the see of Johannesburg. His political astuteness, of course, was very much in evidence during the tumultuous and historic decade he spent as Archbishop of Cape Town, a period that witnessed the release of Nelson Mandela, freedom for South African peoples and the establishment of the Truth and Reconciliation Commission.

To grasp Archbishop Desmond's political awakening we must turn the clock back nearly seven decades to his boyhood in a town called Ezenzeleli where his mother worked as a cook at an institute for the blind. In an address at the first "Naught for Your Comfort" lecture at the Chruch of Christ the King, Sophiatown, he told the story of his first encounter with a white priest of whose identity he was unaware at the time. The priest "swept past my mother and me when I was about nine or ten, and doffed his hat to my mother, a black domestic worker, doing something that was so thoroughly un-South African in those days." Tutu recounts that "that gesture made an indelible impression on me."[177] The priest, of course, was Trevor Huddleston, the English monk who would become Tutu's mentor and a stalwart champion for the rights of black South Africans.

But that random gesture in a township road proved to be but the outward and visible sign of a deeper sense of commitment on Huddleston's part—respect for the people committed to his charge. Tutu further describes Huddleston's care for him during the twenty-month period he was hospitalized with tuberculosis. Tutu comments: "I was quite amazed that someone so important and so busy could have taken the time to visit me . . . an unimportant township urchin. That interest in a nonentity like me taught me profound lessons about the importance of each person, lessons I hope that helped to shape my own ministry."[178] We see in this description of a young Huddleston the seeds of his ministry of selfless service. His acts of defiance against the government were grounded primarily in a love for the people whom he served. Doffing his hat to Mrs. Tutu was an early sign of his devotion to the South African people.

Huddleston's acts struck Desmond Tutu as countercultural. They made a statement that the church's values were different than those of the government's. The government made it very clear that one's worth was dependent upon one's race and class. The church, however, preached that the Kingdom of God embraced all of humanity, even township urchins, and reckoned them to be children of God. These acts proclaimed that the church, represented in these incidents by an Englishman in a flowing white cassock, challenged and defied the mores of the nation in which the church was carrying out its work. These acts signified that "the least, the lost and the last" of South African society had value and meaning in the eyes of the church. In a eulogy at Huddleston's funeral in 1998, Tutu put it this way: "Trevor's theology made it natural to do what was politically and socially unnatural—he had a sense of the infinite value of each individual person." Tutu believed that the church, as the agent of the Kingdom, and as an institution dedicated to upholding the dignity of each human being, would always ultimately trump society. It is understandable, therefore, that it was such a view of the church which later provided the theological rationale for Tutu's involvement in the struggle for South African freedom. "Our skills were honed in that anti-apartheid struggle—as a Church we declared that the Kingdom of God required a free and democratic South Africa where everyone counted."[179]

Johannesburg: Tutu's Boot Camp

My first visit to South Africa was in 1985 for the enthronement of Desmond Tutu as bishop of Johannesburg. With others in the delegation from the Episcopal Church (USA) I joined the colorful procession of mitered bishops and archbishops, greater and lesser prelates, bewigged chancellors, mace-wielding vergers and government officials wearing the insignia of their respective offices. Some in attendance were in somber Western dress, others in vibrant African garb. The liturgy on that February morning in St. Mary's Cathedral was an eclectic blend of standard Anglican worship and distinctly South African traditions. Surpliced choristers rendered psalms in flawless metrical chant, while a choir singing in Xhosa, swaying to the beat of drums, led the congregation in jubilant hymns set to syncopated and ululating rhythms. Needless to say, all the participants were enveloped in "wreaths of incense cloud."

The euphoric atmosphere of that celebration gave few clues to the tense political situation that permeated both church and state during that period. Apartheid was still the law of the land, and police vans were parked outside the Cathedral as an ominous reminder that the police could have arrested the worshippers inside for no other reason than that they participated in an interracial gathering. The world's opposition to and impatience with apartheid were escalating. In 1985, nearly a thousand fatalities were linked to political unrest. For the first time since the Sharpeville massacre of 1960, the government would impose specially enacted emergency laws which would allow police to arrest without warrant and to detain people indefinitely. According to Bishop Peter Lee, there was "near civil-war between the people and the security forces. The Johannesburg area was the eye of the political storm and the churches were in the thick of it."[180] Ninety U.S. firms had ceased to do business in South Africa. Scant weeks before the enthronement, the bishop-elect of Johannesburg, in recognition of "the courage and heroism shown by black South Africans in their use of peaceful methods in the struggle against apartheid," had received the Nobel Peace Prize.

These developments had a decided effect on the life of the church and the process which led to Tutu's appointment as Bishop of Johannesburg. Many feared that Tutu's election might cause the white minority of the diocese to withhold the majority of the funding which it had always provided. Many whites also were afraid that the bishopric would provide for Tutu a "bully pulpit" from which he could continue his ministry of protest. (Most of Tutu's black supporters were delighted at the same prospect, although some were concerned that the visibility of the high post might serve to muzzle him). One priest summarized the church's dilemma by saying, "If it appoints Bishop Tutu, this will be seen as a political appointment; if it doesn't appoint him, it will be seen as a political disappointment."[181]

Unable to resolve these issues, the electoral assembly of the Diocese failed to give Tutu the two-thirds majority required for election. Bishop Peter Lee observes that these justifiable reservations notwithstanding, "there was racism involved in the failure to elect Tutu."[182] After the deadlock, the matter was referred to the synod of bishops of the Province of Southern Africa, who elected Desmond Tutu as bishop of Johannesburg, the first and to date the only black to hold that post. A year and a half later, the church would again be faced "with the prospect of flying in the face of racist ideology and practice by choosing its first black Archbishop of Cape Town,"[183] but on that occasion the electoral process moved with dispatch, and the assembly moved to an almost immediate consensus.

Tutu's inaugural address as Bishop of Johannesburg, delivered as the charge at his enthronement, was in many ways a précis of his theological views. His first point had to do with worship, a worship which has as its end the praise of Almighty God out of which would flow giving, evangelism and intercession, and more especially prayers for peace, justice and reconciliation. "Inspired by our worship and adoration of God and so made sensitive to discover Jesus Christ among the poor, the hungry, the oppressed," he pleaded, "I hope that you will speak out against what causes suffering and anguish to God's children just because they are black." This in turn was linked to his understanding of the church, which he declared was neither a cozy club, nor a mystical ivory tower, nor a spiritual ghetto, nor even a center of good works, but a living organism committed to those at the margins of society. It was in this context, moreover, that he described himself as the pastor who was committed both to Anglicans in the Diocese of Johannesburg as well as to those who have no particular claim on him.

Those who expected him to make "political" statements in that sermon were not to be disappointed, but careful listening would reveal that such politics sprang from his understanding of the nature of the church as a caring community, and of his role as pastor. True to form, his sermon demonstrated that his politics and his Incarnational theology are inseparable. He made a plea for the dismantling of apartheid and vowed (for the first time) to call for punitive economic sanctions in the absence of any signs of such a dismantling. He felt justified in calling for such action because failure to do so would result in the continual suffering of those under the yoke of apartheid.

One of Tutu's favorite stories is of the mouse, the lion and the elephant. The elephant is sitting on the mouse's tail, rendering the tiny creature immobile. A lion comes along, and the mouse entreats him to let out a great roar, which would startle the elephant, thus freeing the mouse. The lion refuses to intercede, and informs the mouse that the problem is one solely between the elephant and the mouse, and is not his affair. The mouse courageously suggests to the king of the jungle that either he is part of the problem, or part of the solution. Although Tutu did not tell that story as part of his sermon, its spirit permeated his remarks. Tutu upbraided those who claimed to be Christian but who raised no protest to "callous and inhumane" actions perpetrated on God's people. Like Amos, Tutu reminded the assembled congregation of the sin of indifference. "The authenticity of a proper religious attitude is tested in concrete ways," he reminded them. "The God of the Bible scandalizes religious people constantly."

Ubuntu: The Driving Force behind Tutu's Theology

To understand the role that Desmond Tutu played in South Africa and his unique contribution to the history of the CPSA, we must grasp that in many ways, the premise of his theology is unique. He rejects pigeon-holing labels, even those considered to be flattering. For example, he once commented, "I don't preach a social gospel; I preach the Gospel, period. The Gospel of our Lord Jesus Christ is concerned with the whole person. When people are hungry, Jesus didn't say, 'Now is that political or social?' He said, 'I feed you.' Because the good news to a hungry person is bread."

Citing Scripture, he turns the rationale of apartheid on its head, asserting that if one's value depends on one's skin color, such a view is contrary to the Scriptures, which say that our value is predicated on our having been created in the image of God.[184] Coupled with his biblical faith is, as we have seen, a formidable ecclesiology. Being in the world but not of it, the church, in order to be effective, must never be neutral, but must maintain a critical distance from political structures so that it can be free to exercise a prophetic ministry. "In a situation of injustice and oppression, such as we have in South Africa, not to choose to oppose is in fact to have chosen to side with the powerful, with the exploiter, with the oppressor."[185] As regards the evil of apartheid, therefore, the church is afforded a unique opportunity. By confronting it, the church does nothing less than "regain integrity and promote the cause of justice and peace."[186]

Tutu brings to his strong Incarnational and ecclesiological emphases a distinctly African approach known as *Ubuntu*. It is roughly translated as "humanity," but it is more than that. "The springboard of Tutu's thinking," according to one of Tutu's biographers, is "the very essence of that mysterious quality which makes a person a person in African understanding."[187] Predicated on a belief in the integrity of creation and the recalling of our image of God in the midst of human conflict, the concept is often described by Tutu in the phrase, "a person is a person through other persons." A glowing coal, says Tutu in a favorite metaphor, loses its heat and, more significantly, its ability to provide warmth when it is separated from other coals and is forced to exist on its own away from the hearth.

Michael Battle further explains *Ubuntu* as a "corrective hermeneutic for Western salvation theology that focuses on the individual."[188] In contrast to a traditional theology which tends to categorize people as good and evil, and in turn asks that evil persons repent of their transgressions, *Ubuntu* asks that the oppressed see in their oppressors (and the oppressors in the oppressed) the image of God. *Ubuntu,* then, introduces the radical concept that all persons, whether oppressed or oppressors, are peers and potential friends, reflective of Jesus' teaching in John 15:15. With both oppressor and oppressed entering into a friendship, they restore humanity to a state that is closer to what God intended in creation. The goal of *Ubuntu* is *koinonia*, or Christian community. Moreover, *Ubuntu* builds on Tutu's Incarnational theology, because only God through Jesus Christ knows suffering through the Crucifixion.[189]

Tutu's *Ubuntu* in action is captured in an excerpt from the presentation speech read at the time of his being awarded the Nobel Prize for Peace:

> A massacre of the black population had just taken place—the camera showed ruined houses, mutilated human beings and crushed children's toys. Innocent people had been murdered. Women and children mortally wounded. But, after the police vehicles had driven away with their prisoners, Desmond Tutu stood and spoke to a frightened and bitter congregation: 'Do not hate,' he said, 'let us choose the peaceful way to freedom.'

I believe that the Nobel committee chose this vignette as emblematic of Tutu's commitment to peace through *Ubuntu*. Given the wanton destruction of life and property wrought by government forces, there might be an expectation that even Christian leaders would be tempted to incite the people to riot, and to urge them to retaliate with violence. But Tutu characteristically eschewed the eye-for-an-eye approach in favor of a turn-the-other-cheek approach, knowing that, ultimately, his methodology would prove more effective.

Such a spirit of *Ubuntu* was a guiding principle for Tutu in his successive roles as Secretary General of the SACC, Bishop of Johannesburg and Archbishop of Cape Town. Tutu saw himself as leading a church guided by the principle of *Ubuntu*. To Tutu, the church is a multifaceted organism. First, it is a worshipping community, whose primary purpose is to praise Almighty God; a servant church, willing to wash the feet of others. Second, it is an inclusive organization, open to all sorts and conditions of men and women. But the church, while functioning in these ways, must also be a suffering servant, willing at all times to take up the Cross and bear the consequences of its prophetic witness. But there was another important aspect of Tutu's

Ubuntu-inspired ecclesiology. In a belief reminiscent of the high doctrine of the church held by Newman, Keble and other Oxford divines, Tutu firmly believed in the church as holy and set apart, and therefore off-limits to outside intervention or control. "No secular authority, not even the government of the land, has any authority to sit in judgment on the churches about how to be church, and how it is to fulfill its God-given mandate to work for the extension of God's kingdom."[190]

Such an ecclesiology informed his leadership style at the SACC, often to the consternation of his staff and the frustration of his constituencies. He firmly believed that in order to make the most impact on society, the SACC could not be seen as a secular body. Tutu inaugurated practices, therefore, to refute the view held by conservative churchmen that "activists in the international ecumenical movement were more concerned with social structures than with their relationship with God." He declared that a disciplined prayer life, Bible study and staff retreats were not peripheral to their work, but central to it. He declared that they must be seen as patterning their lives after Jesus Christ, who was first and foremost a man of prayer.[191] Such practices doubtless caused some of Tutu's critics to sit up and take notice. The ease with which Tutu could move among politicians, government officials, common laborers as well as all sorts and conditions of church folk caused at least one detractor, a priest in the Diocese of Johannesburg, to label him as a clever-dick, worldly, sociopolitical manipulator.[192]

Even a cursory study of Tutu's archiepiscopate reveals how much he relied on his *Ubuntu* theology as a model. While the differences of opinion within the church cannot be compared to the often pitched-battle enmity between pro- and anti-apartheid forces, there were, nevertheless, a plethora of divergent views. Bishop Michael Nuttall commented, "Within the Province, there is the full spectrum of views on virtually every issue. . . . But our strength has been in our ability to hold on to one another despite such differences." He added, "Desmond Tutu's style of leadership has been a major factor in this."[193]

The bishops of the province, for example, were divided on the issue of sanctions, and more specifically, as to whether the CPSA should support economic sanctions against an intractable South African government. Tutu, it will be remembered, in his charge on the occasion of his enthronement as Bishop of Johannesburg, had promised to support such action if there were no signs of the dismantling of apartheid within a year and a half. Just a few months into his archiepiscopate, the clock was ticking loudly, but typically, as Nuttall observes, "he did not attempt to bulldoze his fellow bishops into supporting" his plan. Rather, in the spirit of *Ubuntu,* they "walked the road of a careful wisdom . . . [and] in the end came to an agreement which involved give-and-take on all sides."[194] Specifically the synod of bishops endorsed specific targeted pressures as opposed to indiscriminate comprehensive sanctions.

Another example of his style of leadership was seen in the way that he led the province through the debate on the divisive issue of women's ordination. Mother Vivian Harber, a priest on the staff of St. George's Cathedral, Cape Town, commented with deep appreciation on the archbishop's patience and fairness throughout the whole process. What was abundantly clear was his empathy with those on all sides of the issue. Tutu himself had arrived at the position that the church should move forward to ordain women, but it is noteworthy that his rationale for doing so was not expressed in terms of rights or even justice, but, in keeping with his theology, in terms of what was best for the mission of the church and for the building up of the Christian community. In his charge to the delegates at the 1992 Provincial Synod, he said, "I believe quite firmly that [ordination of women] is God's will for our Church at this time. We will be a more gentle, a more caring Church with women priests, for ordination is not to power or into an elite caste, but it is for service and sacrifice."

Before the vote was taken, Tutu, in a statement fully reflective of his *Ubuntu* theology, announced "We need, under the Spirit's guidance, to be open to one another, to hear what God is saying to us through one another. And every one of us must be free to express exactly what . . . the Holy Spirit of God has convicted them to say."[195] On the morning after the overwhelming vote was taken in favor of ordaining women, Tutu told the delegates that he didn't sleep well the previous night thinking on the one hand about those who would find the decision painful and unacceptable, and on the other those who would find it a cause for rejoicing.[196] Tutu demonstrated through his actions that through *Ubuntu,* each individual felt affirmed, and that there could be friendship even in the throes of vehement disagreement, a principle which more and more became characteristic of his ministry.

Desmond Tutu's *Ubuntu* leadership style is effective because it makes it possible for all parties to be heard. Even those whose positions are not ultimately adopted feel valued as human beings who have had an indispensable role in the process. If indeed one of the definitions of *Ubuntu* is "being a person through other people," this means that one's personhood is upheld and in the final analysis is far more significant than one's opinions.

Tutu as Statesman: Truth and Reconciliation

It is clear that Tutu's *Ubuntu* methodology was especially suited for the position he held after demitting office as archbishop. It was doubtless because of Tutu's demonstrated ability to bring together people of divergent views and to value them as individuals and as children of God that in 1996 President Nelson Mandela appointed him to chair the Truth and Reconciliation Commission. The Commission was mandated to investigate the crimes perpetrated in South Africa during the apartheid regime, especially murder, abduction, torture, and severe ill-treatment, and to provide "as complete a picture as possible of the nature, causes and extent of gross violations of human rights." *Ubuntu* was the philosophical and theological framework which Tutu was able to use to address apartheid's hard truths. Only through such an open process could there be a reconciliation process which in turn could enable the nation to move beyond apartheid's legacy. In describing its work, Tutu stated that "there is a need for understanding but not for vengeance, a need for reparation but not for retaliation, a need for *Ubuntu* but not for victimization."

At another level, Tutu's appointment was a statement about and (although Tutu would not have asked for it) a vindication of the role of the church as a champion of justice. It is a supreme irony that a man whom the government had excoriated for his political involvement and his meddling in the affairs of state should be chosen by the government to be the chief architect of reconciliation in a nation divided and deeply wounded. At the same time, it was a logical choice, since it was Tutu who had emerged, as Ndungane has observed, as "an outstanding leader in the midnight of apartheid in the 1970s," and as one who was able to make it possible for others to see the light at the end of the tunnel.[197] It is for good reason that Bishop Nuttall described Tutu as an "icon of reconciliation."[198]

The Truth and Reconciliation Commission will doubtless go down in history as a twentieth-century miracle. Its birth was an entirely countercultural event. It can be said that it marks the first time in modern history that a nation adopted unadulterated moral principles, predicated on Christian ethics, to redress grievous societal wrongs. In its establishment, South Africa eschewed the statutory and legalistic standards of its own time-honored system of jurisprudence, and replaced them with provisions for amnesty for egregious and heinous acts, even including murder.[199] In exchange for a full and complete disclosure of the facts relevant to the offense, even if no remorse were expressed, the perpetrator would be pardoned. The government, now in the hands of those who, with their families, were the victims of the odious crimes, seemed willing to forego revenge or even the knowledge that "the punishment fit the crime." The government, in its insightful wisdom, understood that the catharsis which the perpetrators endured might in fact be more effective in the long run, and for the eventual soul's health of the nation, than an indeterminate prison sentence or execution. In other words, the new South African government through its actions made the radical statement that in order to be effective, justice need not be retributive, it can be restorative. And for Tutu, *Ubuntu*-inspired restorative justice "reflects a fundamental and venerable African value of healing and nurturing social relationships at the expense of exacting vengeance, of nothing less than a quality of humane sociality."[200]

The Commission made it clear that it was not changing the face of South African jurisprudence forever. The TRC was invented for the particular purpose of hearing cases pertaining to acts committed between the Sharpeville Massacre in 1960 and the inauguration of Nelson Mandela thirty-four years later. "The TRC was an explicit political compromise between the broad amnesty that apartheid leaders sought and the prosecutions proposed by the African National Congress, which would have antagonized any hope of a peaceful transition."[201] The solution, which actually encouraged both confession and transparency, was to keep the prosecution option open but grant individual amnesties for those who came forward and told the truth about their crimes, in public and often on television.

Nevertheless, the Commission's work was severely criticized by many who had been either the perpetrators or victims of apartheid who believed that justice was not being served. Some believed that it opened more old wounds than it healed. Many opposed the idea that amnesty should be granted to any who had been found guilty of human rights violations, even if they apologized publicly. Others objected to the stipulation that amnesty be available only to those who pled guilty, and not to those who claimed to be innocent, as was the case of those who killed Steve Biko.[202] Even Ndungane observed that the Commission's "limited mandate and duration did not allow the Commission to dig deep enough into our past and come up with recommendations that would set the tone for a lasting peace."[203] Nevertheless, the work of the Commission was an important first step in an attempt to assess and redress the devastating effects of the legacy of apartheid. Tutu brought to his role as chairman of the Commission the same understanding of *Ubuntu* which had been the guiding force behind his work of reconciliation within the church as it grappled with issues that had proved to be divisive.

Tutu's *Ubuntu* theology could be consummately effective in addressing the devastation of the nation in the wake of apartheid because everyone—perpetrators and victims alike—was invited to the table to share their pain, their hurt and their anguish. People were understood first to be children of God and were not adjudged, *ipso facto,* as guilty or innocent simply because of the nature of their role in the struggle. Because in *Ubuntu*, the humanity of one person is inextricably caught up in the humanity of everybody else, it provided a common ground from which all participants could begin to move forward. Further, as Tutu has explained, "A person with *Ubuntu* is open and available to others, affirming of others, does not feel threatened" by others. Moreover, in *Ubuntu*, individuals share a common plight with others, even when that means that others are diminished or humiliated.[204] This means that a framework is provided through which perpetrators and victims alike can feel compassion for each other.

Tutu made it clear that the Truth and Reconciliation was a "third way"; it could indeed be seen as an adaptation of the Anglican concept of via media. The Commission would neither follow the pattern of the Nuremberg trials nor would it propose that the best way forward would be for every South African to be afflicted with amnesia.[205] Tutu could adopt such a stance because at the root of his theology is a crucified Jesus who "supports the development of all individuals who are persons, privately, personally, relationally and socially,"[206] Similarly, Tutu as commissioner was not cast in the role of judge or lord high executioner. He assumed the task, as the deputy chair of the Commission described it, as "a wounded healer, not better than anyone else, but simply as [someone] who had been given a job to do and *who cared very deeply for victims and perpetrators alike*."[207]

The Centripetal Force of Forgiveness Overcomes the Centrifugal Force of Alienation

Many critics of the Commission, regardless of where they find themselves on the political or theological spectrum, including some Africans who understand the concept of *Ubuntu* and pattern their lives after it, have failed to grasp the central tenet of Tutu's position. That simple concept, often "hidden in plain sight," is forgiveness. And it is to that theological concept to which Tutu appealed when he accepted President Mandela's appointment as chair of the commission: "True reconciliation is never cheap, for it is based on forgiveness which is costly. Forgiveness in turn depends on repentance, which has to be based on an acknowledgement of what was done wrong, and therefore on disclosure of the truth. You cannot forgive what you do not know."[208]

Tutu claims no pride of authorship for these concepts. He only draws on the principles of moral theology. Repentance (*metanoia* in the New Testament) is the decision to turn around, to make a 180-degree turn, after acknowledging wrongdoing, and to seek amendment of life. Forgiveness is God's assurance that sin has been expunged and the slate wiped clean. It gives the penitent sinner, the one who now admits the truth, a new start. Only then can true reconciliation take place, since the sinner, having received divine pardon, is then free to seek the forgiveness of those persons whom he has offended. This is a costly process, Tutu explains, because it runs counter to the usual disposition of the human psyche, which is caught up in the vortex of a centrifugal force of alienation, brokenness, hostility and disharmony.[209] A centrifugal force is best likened to the action inside the tub of a washing machine, which repels items from the center and pushes them to the outer walls. The penitent must seek instead the centripetal process that moves toward the center, toward unity, harmony, goodness and peace. When we do so, Tutu believes, we re-create Eden, a state symbolic of what God intended for God's creatures.

Such a restoration to God's status quo, however, rarely, if ever, occurs. "True reconciliation," according to Tutu, "exposes the awfulness, the abuse, the pain, the degradation, the truth." He even allows that it is a risky undertaking which could even make things worse. And while it is difficult for the culprit to admit wrongdoing, it is even more difficult for the victim, even allowing for the limits of forgiveness, to forgive the perpetrator of the evil deeds. While forgiveness does not expect victims to forget or condone, and while true forgiveness is never sentimental, it does mean, as Tutu eloquently expresses it, "abandoning your right to pay back the perpetrator in his own coin."[210] But the reconciliation among South Africans incurs an additional price. Tutu maintains that because of the disparities between rich whites and poor blacks which have come about as a result of the inherent injustices in the system, it will be necessary for houses to replace hovels, and for decent education, adequate employment and safe environments to be available before true reconciliation can take place.

The genius of Tutu's *Ubuntu*-inspired theology of forgiveness is its simplicity. He has shown how conflict resolution can be achieved between individuals using Christian principles, and has further demonstrated how such a model can be used to address divergence of opinion in the life of the church as well as in the bosom of the nation. Beyond South Africa's borders, Archbishop Tutu has preached the same sermon, holding up the South African paradigm as an example for other strife-torn nations such as Ireland, Rwanda and Israel. His basic message has been that forgiveness should be held up as an alternative to retribution. He points, for example, to Nelson Mandela who emerged from twenty-seven years' incarceration, "not spewing words of hatred and revenge," but showing himself instead as the "heroic embodiment of reconciliation and forgiveness."[211]

Tutu: An Icon of World Peace

It has been more than twenty years since Desmond Tutu was awarded the Nobel Prize for Peace for his efforts, principally in his capacity of Secretary General of the SACC, to secure freedom in South Africa. As we look back on the conferral of that coveted award, we see it less as a prize for his accomplishments prior to 1984, and more as a prophetic act on the part of the judges in Oslo. It is not an exaggeration to say that Tutu has continued to earn the Prize, first for his involvement in the process which led to the abolition of apartheid in South Africa, and then for his work on the TRC. But history will doubtless record that his greatest accomplishment has been the "domino effect" that the TRC has caused. Although Truth and Reconciliation Commissions first appeared in places like Argentina and Chile to uncover the truth about mass disappearances, "it is South Africa's Commission that, though flawed in many ways, has set a high standard for future commissions."[212]

Since the gavel fell on the South African Commission, other countries, most of them fragile democracies laboring under the administrations of transitional governments, were encouraged by the outcome in South Africa and established commissions of their own. Among them are Guatemala, Haiti, Nigeria, Philippines, Sierra Leone, and East Timor.[213]

Each of these nations has picked up the baton and carried it in an international relay race for freedom. They have learned from the suffering of the South African people. But they have also learned from their redemption and vindication, a course of events inspired in no small measure by the Anglican Church there, and its primate, a plucky, diminutive man who had the temerity first to declare to the government that apartheid is sin, and further to preside over a process which provided a means for forgiveness and reconciliation. The debt that the world owes to Archbishop Tutu and the Anglican Church in South Africa is incalculable.

Chapter VI

A Prophet without Honor?
The Visionary Ministry of
Njongonkulu Winston Hugh
Ndungane

*Njongo is a prophet, but he is also a wise politician. He is not
afraid to point out the errors the church has made. He is not
afraid to bravely speak the truth to the powerful. His motto is
"All for Christ, and Christ for all."*

—Thabo Makgoba
Bishop of Grahamstown[214]

Pontifex Africanus

Archbishop Ndungane's charge, delivered to the 31st Synod of the CPSA
in July 2005, was entitled "Building Bridges of Hope." The choice of the
theme was not coincidental. Ndungane sees himself as pontifical, in the true
sense of the word of being a bridge builder. In his charge, he called upon
Anglicans in the CPSA to "build bridges of God's hope in the world." In
his address, he calls Jesus "God's bridge of hope to God's world . . . who
bridges the unbridgeable," and who "is the bridge of hope for the poor—
whether poor materially, emotionally, or spiritually." He therefore challenges
the church to be like Jesus, a bridge who offered the gift of hope "to those on
the other side—the excluded, the marginalized, the outcast, the unclean, the

despised, the rejected."[215] For Ndungane, the Church, the Body of Christ, is the bridge by means of which the world can be reached. He believes that by virtue of his office, he is the bridge builder, called to lead the people of God to cross a bridge which traverses a chasm of despair. Such a vision is central to Ndungane's theology, and grasping it provides us with a lens through which we can more fully understand his ministry.

The bridge-building theme peppers Ndungane's statements and is never far from any of his acts as archbishop. In a letter to the chairman and CEO of Pfizer, Inc., in March, 2000, in which he addressed the HIV/AIDS pandemic in South Africa, and particularly the question of making drugs available and affordable to those who are infected, the archbishop wrote that the church was in a unique position to find a way to "bridge the gulf between human needs, scientific effort and market returns."[216] In 2003, the archbishop reported that Robert Mugabe, President of Zimbabwe, had invited the CPSA to help bridge the gulf between Harare and London to resolve the country's economic and political problems, for which Mugabe has publicly blamed the British government. Ndungane met with Mugabe at a meeting at which Molefe Tsele, SACC President, was also in attendance.[217] Ndungane's intervention in this matter, including his willingness to convey Mugabe's concerns to the Archbishop of Canterbury, speaks highly of the respect which the CPSA and its primate, and indeed South Africa itself, command both in England and in sister countries on the African continent.

In March of 2004, Archbishop Ndungane met with Archbishop Akinola of Nigeria, at which time the two primates discussed their divergent views on the consecration of an openly gay bishop in the American Church, and how this would affect Anglican unity. They reached a concordat of sorts, in which the two primates agreed to work together to strengthen the position of the church in Africa on the issue of human sexuality; to collaborate with African political leaders on conflict prevention; and to join forces to eradicate poverty and diseases, especially HIV/AIDS. The significance of this meeting and the document it produced cannot be overemphasized. It serves as a reminder that although the Western press would suggest that the overarching issue for the African churches is human sexuality, the African leaders themselves are deeply concerned with the life-and-death issues that impact their daily existence. Moreover, they are willing to lay aside issues which serve as a detraction to the accomplishment of the church's mission.

In commenting on the meeting, the bishop of Grahamstown said of his archbishop: "Njongo is concerned about the question of collegiality with his fellow bishops in Africa, and does not want any of them to be ostracized from each other. Therefore he tried to stress those issues that they had in common. He is a bridge-builder."[218]

Significantly, Ndungane sees the people of the CPSA as a bridge not only to the "least, the lost and the last" in South Africa, but to fellow Anglicans beyond South Africa's borders; indeed he believes that the South African church can act both as mediator and sounding board for the entire Anglican Communion. He believes this to be the case because of South Africa's unique experience as a nation and as a Christian community. Its multicultural society and its role in the dismantling of apartheid uniquely fit the South African church to serve as exemplar for the entire Anglican Communion. In a reference to the ongoing debate on human sexuality, for example, he made it clear that the CPSA need not adopt others' agendas, or feel duty bound to walk in lockstep with other churches either in Africa or in the West. "As we pursue the Lambeth Resolution and study the Windsor report, we are not bound to engage with them according to the terms of other people's battles. Indeed, I will go further: we must not allow ourselves to be dictated to by the agendas of other parts of the Communion. On the contrary, we can be a bridge of hope to them."[219] He believes, too, that Anglicans from Africa and from the African diaspora are especially called to a pontifical ministry. In July, 2005, in a sermon preached in Toronto at the opening Eucharist of the third International Conference on Afro-Anglicanism, he declared "We have a potential to build a bridge within the Anglican Communion. What we have in common is far greater than what divides us."

In that sermon, Ndungane, speaking to an audience made up largely of members of the African diaspora, remarked: "I have been pondering what it means to be an Afro-Anglican . . . because identity is a fundamental marker of ourselves. People taken from their homes have a unique journey to find an authentic past to call one's own."[220] He was suggesting that Anglicans of color in general, and South Africans in particular, have much to offer the entire Anglican Communion. He is saying that those who have been wrested from their own soil (whether taken across the ocean or into a "homeland") and have been stripped of their identities have been strengthened through such adversity for service to the church and the world. Such a gift, despite its origin, is something which Africans proudly offer to their brother and sister Anglicans.

In a very real sense, Archbishop Ndungane sees the church as the agency best equipped to be a bridge over which the disadvantaged may travel to economic security. He believes that the church, to be true to its calling, must be committed to seeing that every human being fulfills his or her potential as God intended, and having done so, must ensure that each person whose life is touched by the church must be equipped for service. As he so eloquently expressed it in his charge to Synod, "As bridge builders, we need to be master masons who train others in the same craft." He sees the church as fulfilling the prophecy of Isaiah (65:20–22):

> No more shall there be in it an infant that lives but a few days, or an old person who does not live out a lifetime; for one who dies at a hundred years will be considered a youth, and one who falls short of a hundred will be considered accursed. They shall build houses and inhabit them; they shall plant vineyards and eat their fruit. They shall not build and another inhabit; they shall not plant and another eat; for like the days of a tree shall the days of my people be, and my chosen shall long enjoy the work of their hands.

Poverty: The New Apartheid

Ndungane sees the relevance of this text for today's world. These verses speak of an end to infant mortality, of the availability of health care for all and the promise of a dignified old age. He sees a nation which offers secure housing and economic stability, where everyone may safely enjoy the fruit of their labors, in peace and joy.[221] Ndungane's vision of a South Africa where such salubrious conditions obtain is, of course, in contrast to the current reality. This is why when, in an interview with the archbishop I asked him to name the most significant problem facing South Africa today, he without any hesitation identified poverty. The demographic statistics are inordinately affected by poverty and AIDS, which infects 21% of the population. The infant mortality rate is 58 per 1,000 live births, and life expectancy at birth is 43 years. The economic picture is grim. Fifty percent of the people live below the poverty line, and the unemployment rate is 26%. The bottom 10%

of the population receive 1% of the income, and the top 10% receive 46%.[222] Adjustments made for ethnicity would reveal that principally owing to the legacy of apartheid, black South Africans are disproportionately poorer, and have higher rates of AIDS infection, infant mortality and unemployment, and have a shorter life span.[223]

To Ndungane, poverty is not simply an economic condition characterized by a lack of resources. "It is insidious and diabolical," he writes—insidious because it is not seen in the stark terms of racial discrimination; diabolical because those with power and wealth often refuse to recognize the inequities imposed on the poor."[224] Poverty is also, as Ndungane understands it, a theological problem, because it diminishes the image of God in the eyes of the poor and prevents them from having life and having it abundantly (John 10:10). But poverty is no less a theological problem for the rich, who too often, out of greed or complacency, fail to do the justice necessary to alleviate poverty. To Ndungane, poverty is, therefore, more than a lamentable condition; it is intrinsically evil. He has even called it "the new global apartheid" because, like racial apartheid, it is rooted in the accidents of birth. It is impossible, therefore, to bring the message of hope which the Gospel proclaims to people without first tackling the poverty which defines their existence.

At the thirteenth Lambeth Conference in 1998, Archbishop Ndungane took a leading role in addressing this global apartheid, which has come about and continues unchecked largely because of the massive debt which developing countries owe to the world's richest nations. He observed that for every dollar ($1US) that rich countries lend to developing countries, eleven dollars comes straight back in the form of repayment on debts owed to the rich countries.[225] As I point out elsewhere, this debt seems even more extreme and unreasonable because for centuries developed nations in Europe wrested both natural and human resources from developing countries, especially in Africa; now those industrialized nations, making no allowance for the fact that they achieved their wealth largely at the expense of the debtor nations, are lending money to their former colonies at exorbitant rates of interest.[226] This global reality, in turn, exacerbates the already abject poverty of South African blacks, since it means that the nation's economy, indebted to richer nations, has less capital to use to ameliorate the wretched conditions in which the poor find themselves.

Ndungane was one of the bishops who made an impassioned plea not merely for the reduction of world debt, but, in the spirit of the Old Testament concept of jubilee, for its remission. In expounding on this biblical foundation for such a plan in the twenty-fifth chapter of Leviticus, he comments that to bring about a just order in society, we should review our social, political and property arrangements between the poor and the powerful, to ensure that greed and accumulation not go too far before limits are placed on them.[227]

To Ndungane, therefore, the burden of the debt of poor nations resulted not merely in developing countries having less of this world's goods and services. He expressed the dilemma in graphic terms at a meeting of the Primates in 2001. He described the debt borne by developing countries as a "situation that today binds debtor to creditor, that starves the children, that destroys nature, that oppresses women, that keeps people with dark skin at the bottom of the global ladder."[228] Ndungane believes the church can play an essential role in alleviating this problem because it embraces a different moral imperative. "In a world governed and dominated by Mammon, only amongst the faith communities does there seem to be any will to challenge Mammon. Only in our churches . . . does it seem possible to envision a different world and a different economy."[229] This, of course, speaks to Ndungane's belief in the church as a bridge for the poor.

Archbishop Ndungane is passionate about the twin challenges of poverty and hunger. Addressing the "Hunger No More" convocation in Washington in June, 2005, he implored the faith community to help ensure that "the plight of the hungry must not be left for heaven." In September 2005, Archbishop Ndungane participated in a three-day interfaith vigil at the United Nations headquarters in New York City, at which he asked U.S. leaders to increase aid to fight global poverty and to fulfill its commitment to the Millennium Development Goals (MDGs), an eight-prong UN program of which eradication of extreme poverty and hunger by 2015 is the first.[230] Earlier in the same week, Ndungane joined a consultation of international religious leaders who delivered a consensus statement to the United Nations which reaffirmed support for the MDGs and called for increased collaboration between churches and governments in tackling global poverty.

Although Ndungane challenged the governments of industrialized nations to take a lead in this initiative, principally through designating large chunks of their respective budgets to help eliminate the root causes of poverty, he made it clear that the church, as a bridge, has a special role, which stems less from economic power and more from the power of moral suasion. Reminding his listeners that the eradication of poverty was at the top of Jesus' agenda when he set out his priorities for ministry in his sermon in the Temple (Luke 4:18–21), he said, "Churches and other faith communities, which in many countries have a more comprehensive civil society network than any other body, must be leaders in mobilizing public opinion to support the campaigns to 'Make Poverty History' as one slogan has it."[231]

Ndungane believes that for Christians, building a bridge to the poor is not an option. It is the church's primary task at this juncture in our history. Pointing out that morally righteous people have at different times fought against slavery and apartheid and have won, he challenges the church to "combat the scourges of poverty, which Mahatma Gandhi called the deadliest form of violence. Seldom," said Ndungane, "has the church been so challenged in terms of prophetic ministry."[232]

In an attempt to meet that challenge, Ndungane convened a planning meeting in March 2005 which resulted in a call to action for all Anglicans in the province. The CPSA committed itself to improving levels of education; making public services accessible to the poor; tackling HIV/AIDS, malaria and other infectious diseases, and implementing the Millennium Development Goals. To implement these suggestions, a human development fund was established to strengthen the infrastructure and capacity in the poorer dioceses; a poverty and development training course was developed. Finally partnerships between faith based communities and government, business and civil society will be encouraged.[233] The convening of this committee is consistent with Ndungane's style. He mobilizes support around particular justice issues about which he is particularly passionate. His archiepiscopal *imprimatur* confers official status on the project in question, and the impression that he has garnered widespread support. Canon Pato observes, for example, that the CPSA appears to be a united corporate voice, but in fact it tends to be driven by a person at its head, the archbishop. Behind that official corporate voice, he opines, there are many dissenting voices.[234]

Building Bridges to those Living With AIDS

On World AIDS Day, 1 December 2002, Archbishop Ndungane issued this statement: "We need to shout from the rooftops that AIDS is not God's punishment of the wicked. It is a virus and not a sin, and the stigma that society has created around the epidemic is causing people to die instead of living positively." Indeed, Ndungane has suggested that the stigma attached to AIDS may be a greater problem than the disease itself. "As well as the death and devastation the disease leaves in its wake, there is a more insidious problem to overcome—stigma."[235] The Archbishop also believes that the church is in part to be held responsible for such rampant stigmatization. He maintains that in addition to being guilty of perpetuating a theology of a punitive and vindictive God, "we as churches have got funny theologies of prosperity: 'If God loves you, all goes well with you.' We are challenging the Christian communities that HIV/AIDS is not a punishment from God. It is a disease, like any disease: a disease that is manageable, a disease that is treatable."[236] Ndungane believes, therefore, that the church should divert its energy, using it to fight AIDS and not to perpetuate the stigma surrounding it. Churches not willing to make that transition, he maintains, "will have some answering to do on Judgment Day."[237]

Canon Desmond Lambrechts, director of AIDS Ministries for the Province of Southern Africa, is the person principally responsible for carrying out the church's work in this vital area. He faces a daunting task. In a country in which more than ten million people are infected with the HIV virus, some six hundred daily succumb to AIDS. Throughout the province, the church has been involved at a hands-on level. The largest initiative is a partnership between the CPSA and Christian Aid, which is funded by the British government's Department for International Development. One of the realized aims of the project is to have an AIDS coordinator in each of the twenty-three dioceses in the CPSA to provide educational activities. The program, called "Isiseko Sokomeleza" (Building a Foundation) seeks to decrease the incidence of HIV/AIDS, increase the number of people who know their HIV-status, and care for those children living with, orphaned or made vulnerable by HIV/AIDS. The involvement of the local parish in this initiative is imperative to its success. In the Diocese of Johannesburg, for example, HIV counseling and testing centers, operated by an AIDS-awareness group called New Start, are operative in seventy-five parishes.

Through such programs, Ndungane hopes to reverse the church's slow and often inept response to the AIDS crisis. He maintains that the church's reluctance to be an advocate for those living with HIV/AIDS is in part a manifestation of the fact that historically, the church has never been good at dealing sensibly with sex, and has often condemned sexual sin as the worst sin, and those who are infected as if they deserved it. Also, since on the African continent the population most likely to have the disease and to be stigmatized because of it are poor women, the archbishop believes that the patriarchalism and classism ingrained in the church's life make it difficult for it to step in and help.[238]

Ndungane has been personally involved in the church's attempt to educate the public about HIV/AIDS. Fully cognizant of the fact that there is often a credibility gap between church leaders and the general public, Ndungane decided to be tested for AIDS. He could well have had his personal physician visit him at Bishopscourt, and later issued a press release with the results. But he chose instead to take the test in a crowded clinic in one of the townships, and relied on "bush radio" to do the rest.[239] It was in this spirit that he drove home the urgency of the crisis, when addressing a national gathering of the Mothers' Union: "If you feel I am on a soapbox, you are absolutely right. I know with every fibre of my body that we cannot afford to waste time – none of us, not you nor I."[240]

While Ndungane is quick to challenge the church to do its part in the AIDS crisis, he is cognizant of the fact that the church cannot do it alone. In his role as a prophet, the Archbishop of Cape Town has been outspoken in his challenge to the government as well. At a rally in Cape Town on World AIDS Day he said that he was at a loss over government's "endless stalling" when it comes to dealing with the AIDS pandemic, currently affecting an estimated five million South Africans, more than ten percent of the population. He even went so far as to declare that the government of South Africa was sinning against God as well as violating the constitution by denying life-saving drugs to women and children with AIDS.[241] Reminding the government that the "granite wall" of apartheid had collapsed after years of fighting, he asked the government to "turn its undivided attention to AIDS, and to the poverty that exacerbates the disease." Comparing South Africa to developing countries where a great deal has been done to control the spread of AIDS, he called the escalating death rate from AIDS in his country "an unnecessary death sentence." In putting in perspective the number of persons who die from AIDS daily on a global basis, he said it was equivalent to three 9/11s a day. "Such," said Ndungane, "is the terrorism of poverty."[242]

A Conference on Prophetic Witness, Social Development and HIV and AIDS

In the spring of 2005, Ndungane called together a group of church leaders from the United States and South Africa and charged them with the responsibility of planning a conference. It would replace the Gathering that he had hoped would take place in conjunction with the Lambeth Conference in Cape Town, and function as a sequel to a conference on poverty held in South Africa in 2001. Our committee met in Washington and subsequently at Bishopscourt in Cape Town, and christened the conference TEAM (Towards Effective Anglican Mission). It took place in March 2007 at a conference center in Boksburg, near the Johannesburg airport. It was clear that the archbishop wanted this to be a people's conference. In his opening remarks, delivered a fortnight after the adjournment of the meeting of the Primates of the Anglican Communion, he said, "I am extremely delighted to recognize that this is not a gathering of the high and mighty, who in their pomp and glory, tend to pontificate to little tangible effect about solutions for the very complex issues we face in our world."

To Ndungane, the conference was authenticated by the fact that there were in attendance people living with AIDS, people who were poverty-stricken, and people suffering discrimination and various forms of exclusion. Emphasizing that this would not be a conference to philosophize about issues facing the church, he also pointed out that among the attendees were development practitioners committed to the eradication of poverty. He also clarified at the outset that this meeting, which addressed how the church can partner with world organizations to implement the Millennium Development Goals, would demonstrate that the church is concerned with matters other than human sexuality.

Citing the principle of Mutual Responsibility and Interdependence articulated at the 1963 Anglican Congress in Toronto, Ndungane, in an appeal consistent with his commitment to bridge-building, rallied those in attendance to a "deep, prayerful and sacrificial commitment to sharing together in Christ's mission." Invoking the theology of the South African missiologist David Bosch, the archbishop iterated that mission must be understood as an activity that transforms reality. He therefore urged the church to take action to bring about "a new morality for our global village—one that equally values every child of God upon this planet."

Women and Africa: A Shared Plight

Closely related to the issues of poverty and AIDS is the question of the status of women in South African society, and Ndungane has been a staunch and persistent advocate for their cause. In a paper delivered during the celebration of the Centenary of the Women's Union in South Africa,[243] he reminded his audience that three-quarters of women in sub-Saharan Africa between the ages of fifteen and twenty-four are infected with AIDS, and that in some countries, faithful married women (who are infected by their husbands) are at particularly high risk. The situation is compounded by the inability of such women to share their status with their husbands, for fear of being labeled promiscuous, which may further result in their losing the father's financial support of their children or worse, being ostracized from the community entirely. The archbishop points out that although Jesus accorded to women a dignity that was rare in his day, church and society have eschewed his "feminist" theology, and, taking patriarchy as a given, have opted instead to mistreat and marginalize women. He calls this a spiritual blindness toward women. Such attitudes are by no means peculiar to the African continent, but the abject poverty in which so many African women live makes them more vulnerable to subjugation. He calls upon men to use their superior strength to protect and not abuse women, and to accord them the dignity they deserve.

Ndungane understands the problem to have its roots in the church itself, which has been complicit in sustaining the patriarchal dominance of men and the subjugation of women in terms of politics, economics, culture, society and the family as well as within the institutional church. He believes that rather than allowing the church to perpetuate such attitudes, we should instead follow the example of Jesus who challenged the mores of his society and exalted the position of women in his society, making them heralds, evangelists and disciples. One way to do this, according to Ndungane, is to not let HIV/AIDS become a "women's issue" but an issue faced by both men and women.

The Archbishop of Cape Town ingeniously ties together the respective fates of Africa and her women. Women, to Ndungane, have become emblematic of the oppression that besets the continent. We cannot read his words without being struck by the impression that world debt, poverty, AIDS and the oppression of women are not discrete problems, but various aspects of the same phenomenon. He writes: "As patriarchy has devalued women and taught them that they are of less worth then men, so too colonialism taught Africans that their traditions and culture were uncivilized and unchristian."[244]

Believing that dignity must be restored both to African women and to Mother Africa, Ndungane sees hope for the future of church and society in the South African churchwoman. For the great paradox of South African life is that women, though demeaned and marginalized in society, are a force to be reckoned with in the church. To a larger extent than is true elsewhere in Christendom, church life in African Anglicanism is dominated by women— lay women. Despite (to date) an all-male episcopate and an overwhelmingly male priesthood, women are the backbone of the church, in terms of its financial support and its mission. Ndungane is fully aware of this fact, and that is why he has entrusted them with carrying out his most important initiatives, the eradication of AIDS. In an address to the Mother's Union, comprised of strong women many of whom are "already bowed by the curse of HIV/AIDS," and who are burying their children and finding they must look after their grandchildren: "Our Mother's Union has the muscle to make governments and big business sit up. Within your own communities I know there is need for home nursing services, education and huge doses of old fashioned love. In your own homes, your influence is immeasurable. It is from our Mothers that we absorb our values and measure our self worth."[245]

The fact that the archbishop has heaped such praise on the Mother's Union at the same time that he enlists their support reminds us of just how vital to church life this organization is. It is virtually impossible to understand church life in South Africa and other provinces in the developing world without grasping its importance. It was founded in England 125 years ago, as an organization committed to upholding strong family values. As Philip Turner has observed, "It proved an important ally in reshaping sexual mores, and especially in Africa, it became a strong force in undermining traditional understandings of women's roles in favor of replicating the values prevalent in the Church of England at the time of its founding."[246]

In 2004, it celebrated its centenary in South Africa, in commemoration of which Canon Livingstone Ngewu, former rector of the College of the Transfiguration, has recently completed a history. At a recent MU gathering in the Diocese of Port Elizabeth, a guest speaker spoke on the relevance of strong MU branches being needed in South Africa today, saying, "Family life forms the nucleus of the nation. We do not have a safe nation at present as the challenges we face are those of crime, domestic violence and rape of our children. The role of the MUCFL (Mother's Union Christian Family Life) is to stay relevant to the challenges of our community."[247]

Until relatively recently, membership was open only to married women (divorcees were expressly barred from membership) who were mothers of legitimate children. Now boasting 3.5 million members in seventy-six countries, it is open to all women, as well as to men and children. It carries out an extensive program of outreach and development throughout the world. Programs in parenting, nutrition and counseling are among its projects, initiated both by the headquarters in London and by local chapters. Because of stringent standards, membership (by definition devoid of the stigma of out-of-wedlock children) became in many places a status symbol. My own family's roots are in Barbados, where the MU was (and is) very strong. In many parishes there, and elsewhere in the West Indies and in Africa, as well as in many predominantly West Indian parishes in the US, MU members often wear distinctive uniforms (usually white dresses and special sashes) and sit in a body during worship.

There is no doubt that Archbishop Ndungane believes that the hope for Africa resides in the strength and dedication of its women. He believes that women, who consistently manage to overcome adversity for the sake of improving the quality of life for their families, have unique gifts to offer, and one of them is the gift of their power. But he explains that the power of women is not the kind of power which men wield in the spheres of politics, society and the church. "It is the power which Jesus himself endorsed. It is the power of love."[248]

A Twenty-first Century Primate

When Njongonkulu Ndungane, Bishop of Kimberly and Kuruman, was elected in 1996 to succeed Desmond Tutu as Archbishop of Cape Town, a cartoon appeared in a national newspaper. The new archbishop was caricatured wearing a miter which was several sizes too big. It fell down over his eyes and ears. A kindhearted parishioner is also in the cartoon, and she is saying to Ndungane, "Don't worry, Your Grace, it will fit in time."[249] The cartoon captured a not uncommon sentiment that the new Archbishop of Cape Town would be overshadowed by the reputation of his predecessor, the man widely acclaimed as the dismantler of apartheid, an international figure with one of the most recognizable visages on the planet, who had won the Nobel Peace Prize, and who, though diminutive in stature, was larger than life! Even Ndungane confessed that he often said that he pitied the man who would succeed Desmond Tutu.

The cartoon, however, expresses an unfair sentiment, namely that Tutu's successor should fit into his mold. In the decade that has passed since the beginning of Ndungane's archiepiscopate, it has become abundantly clear that he has been fitted for his own miter and wears it very well. He brings his unique gifts to the office which are in turn a product of his own experience. Indeed it can be argued that each page in his life's history has prepared him, each in its own way, for this current chapter. His passion for the poor, the marginalized and the oppressed springs at least in part from his own childhood. Ndungane was born in 1941 in Kokstad, an agricultural center on the slopes of the picturesque Drakensberg mountains in the eastern Province of KwaZulu Natal, about 225 km southwest of Durban. The son and grandson of Anglican priests, he saw firsthand how his father, who was only allowed to minister to black congregations, was forced to work for a fraction of what white clergy received, and how his family's living conditions were far inferior to those of his father's white counterparts. He observed, too, the discriminatory practices under which black Anglicans suffered. Black clergy were effectively silenced in the councils of the church, and at celebrations of the Holy Eucharist which took place during synod, blacks were expected to receive communion after the whites had done so.

The virtual ease with which Ndungane challenges government and those in authority is understandable in light of the skills he learned as a prisoner on Robben Island. At the age of nineteen, he was inspired by a speech he heard by Robert Mangaliso Sobukwe, leader of the Pan Africanist Congress of Azania (PAC). Sobukwe's eloquence, decisiveness and charisma caught the future archbishop's imagination. He felt that he had to stand up and be counted, and to that end began his "long walk in the quest for justice and struggle for liberation." A career in political activism ensued, in which Ndungane went about the business of raising people's consciousness about the evils of apartheid through making speeches and distributing literature. This led to his arrest in 1963, and a three-year sentence on Robben Island. The archbishop observes that although the inmates came from a broad spectrum of political parties, there were excellent relationships among them, because they had a common enemy. Indeed he wishes that a like sense of cooperation existed today, which would assist immeasurably in the challenge of nation building and the eradication of poverty, HIV/AIDS and inequalities of every kind.

The Reverend Canon Luke Pato, Healing and Reconciliation Officer of the South African Council of Churches, has also served as Rector of the College of the Transfiguration in Grahamstown and Provincial Executive Officer for the CPSA. He describes Archbishop Ndungane as passionate about the causes that he espouses. We have already seen how passionate he is about eradicating poverty and AIDS, and about the plight of African women. A former principal of St. Bede's Theological College in Umtata, Ndungane is passionate about theological education, because he is convinced that only through the preparation of qualified, dedicated clergy can the church expect to be equal to the task of being an institution equipped to minister to a changing society. "A Church that does not prepare its leadership adequately for the future," he reminded the Synod in 2004, "dies on its feet." Given the new challenges facing church leaders in the twenty-first century, theological education must keep apace, providing adequate training for men and women "who are able to perceive and respond effectively to the major trends shaping the future." The archbishop's views here are consonant with concerns raised by the Anglican Consultative Council and the Primates of the Communion, who have established TEAC (Theological Education in the Anglican Communion). The group recognizes that there is a distinctive Anglican approach to theological study, reflected in the way Anglican belief is grounded in liturgy and Scripture, but which also respects the need for exploration and experiment and for local traditions and customs.[250]

Ndungane's Vision for the Communion

Ndungane subscribes to the maxim, "Think globally, act locally." So while he is committed to enhancing the quality of life in his own province, he is no less passionate about the Anglican Communion of which it is a part. His campaign against AIDS as well as his support of Bishop Gene Robinson have endeared him to the liberal leadership of the American Episcopal Church. The Province of Southern Africa now enjoys a companion relationship with the Diocese of Washington, which, together with the Dioceses of Southern Ohio and Long Island and Trinity Parish, New York City, have supported CPSA initiatives. English dioceses and organizations (whose support for South Africa had their roots in the anti-apartheid days of Trevor Huddleston) have funneled considerable financial support, much of it earmarked for the fight against AIDS. Ndungane has, of course, predictably, run afoul of most of the African leadership and of conservatives in the West.

His vision for the whole Communion, it should be pointed out, bears virtually no resemblance to a top-down organization, its head office in London, receiving reports from its worldwide outposts. He laments that "part of the story of our Anglican Communion [has been that] the quest for conformity of doctrine and belief and practice—laudable though all three of these may be—has too often involved those at the center of the Communion being sent out to the kraals and villages of far-flung places to correct perceptions and frankly to tell others how things must be with and for them."[251] To Ndungane, therefore, the autonomy of each province is sacrosanct (a principle established by the first Lambeth Conference). To him, autonomy means that each province knows best what is good for the soul's health of its people. This, indeed, was the central theme of Ndungane's remarks regarding the election of the Reverend Canon V. Gene Robinson in the Diocese of New Hampshire. His statement on that election had little to do with the matter of human sexuality, and much more to do with the question of church polity. It can be seen as a virtual compendium of his understanding of the Communion. In it, he makes the following points:

1. The Anglican Communion has no system of centralized government, but is a federation of thirty-eight autonomous ecclesiastical provinces bound together by bonds of affection.

2. When a province disregards a decision of Lambeth, that is regrettable, but it does not mean that the province has acted uneconomically.

3. The Archbishop of Canterbury has no judicial authority over provinces.

4. One of the greatest strengths of Anglicanism is creative diversity.[252]

Ndungane, a graduate of King's College, London, and a frequent lecturer in the United States, Australia and elsewhere, sees the Anglican Communion as a multicultural communion, and not a bastion of British-ness. He has observed that despite Anglicanism's claim to value and embrace diversity, the recent Lambeth Conference, with its bitter controversies around issues of human sexuality and the interpretation of scripture, suggest that we are actually struggling to recognize our diversity, let alone to embrace it.[253] "The marks of our church," according to Ndungane, "are grace, tolerance, and living with difference. We need to make a distinction between issues that are fundamental to the faith and second-order issues. [Human sexuality] is not a church-dividing issue."[254]

In expressing these sentiments, Ndungane echoes the views of Luke Pato, long an advocate of indigenization of the African church, who wrote, "I believe that the time is ripe for the church in Africa in general and the CPSA in particular to make rich contributions to Christianity, and indirectly enrich Anglicanism."[255] Such a desire motivated Ndungane, as Provincial Executive Officer, to invite his fellow members of the Anglican Consultative Council to Cape Town in 1993, in order that they could experience firsthand the vibrancy and diversity of the South African church. And this is why he envisioned a Lambeth Conference in Cape Town. As we have pointed out, the Cape Town Lambeth would have been distinctly different from previous conferences, since Ndungane was also making plans for an Anglican Gathering to be held in conjunction with it. Clergy and laypersons would also be invited to the Gathering as an outward and visible sign that the Anglican Communion is not governed solely by bishops. "Is it right," he asks, "in a Communion claiming to advocate democratic structures that we only invite bishops to consult on the great matters of the day?"[256]

As Archbishop of Cape Town at a time when the Province of Southern Africa has just celebrated its sesquicentennial, Njongonkulu Ndungane has a task before him that is unlike that of any of his predecessors. The residents of Bishopscourt during the twentieth century faced a visible foe—apartheid. Ndungane's foes are of two kinds. Apartheid has in many ways been replaced by poverty, which the Archbishop has called "the new apartheid." Closely linked with poverty is the HIV/AIDS endemic. The imminent danger and supreme irony is that South Africa which has lived to see the dismantling of apartheid runs the risk of being too poor and/or too sick to experience much less enjoy its newfound freedom. Deaths from AIDS threaten to claim the very generation that would be the chief beneficiaries of South African independence. Reminding the South African people that they had fought apartheid "until its granite wall collapsed," he challenged them to do likewise to eradicate HIV/AIDS.[257]

Another, more elusive foe is culture itself, so ingrained in the fabric of society that its presence, if it is understood at all, is not questioned. As Pato observes, the CPSA "owes its greatest debt in terms of its origins, self-understanding, constitutional shape, and even much of its spirituality, to Robert Gray, the first Bishop of Cape Town, a British missionary."[258] Like other Victorian missionaries, Gray believed in an alliance between empire and mission, and that therefore English spirituality would be the vehicle for the spread of the Gospel, and England would remain home, and South Africa a mission field.[259] But now that the Union Jack and apartheid have both come down, there has taken place a major paradigm shift. The challenge before the church is nothing less than the carving out of its new identity. And for this purpose, the Primate of Southern Africa, to be effective, must be countercultural.

Njongonkulu Ndungane, in his desire for a broad-tented church in which believers of various stripes can live in harmony, is engaged in a countercultural ministry. In the decade he has served as primate of the CPSA, he has dared to question some of those characteristics which were part and parcel of a colonial church and society. The perceptions that African culture has no value, that the lot of Africans is to suffer economically while colonial powers prosper, that women are intrinsically inferior, and even that epidemics should be allowed to spread because African life is dispensable must now all be challenged. It is not surprising, therefore, that the outspoken archbishop is perceived by many as having sold out to the West.

The church that emerges from this process will be one that is authentic, reflective of the heritage of its people, emboldened to confront authority, and unafraid to incorporate indigenous expression into its life and worship. Njongonkulu Ndungane, like the importunate widow (Luke 18:1–8) who conducted a sit-in at the judge's chambers, demanding justice, has been assiduous, nay relentless in his determination to raise the questions. History will show to what extent both church and society were willing to heed his clarion call.

Chapter VII

An Iconic Issue:
Human Sexuality
and the CPSA

The Anglican Communion is in crisis. The Episcopal Church in America and the Canadian Anglican Church have broken ranks with other Anglican provinces. The Episcopalians have consecrated as a bishop Gene Robinson, a gay man living openly with a male partner. The Canadian Diocese of New Westminster has agreed to bless same-sex unions. All of this has happened despite a Lambeth Conference agreement that at this time Anglican provinces would not do either of these things.

— Professor Ron Nicolson
School of Religion & Theology,
University of KwaZulu-Natal[260]

The Lambeth Resolution and the South African Response

Professor Nicolson summarizes the current crisis in Anglicanism clearly and succinctly. Devoid of theological arguments on the one hand, and vitriol on the other, the statement allows us to see the problem in stark relief. We understand at once that the nature of the Anglican Communion has been called into question, that the "bonds of affection" among the provinces have been severely strained by the actions of two provinces. While there has never been an understanding that each province in the Communion should always walk in lockstep with the others (indeed, if anything, a contrary understanding has held sway since the first Lambeth Conference), it is clear that recent developments have raised the question as to the extent to which provinces can be out of step with the majority while still professing themselves to be Anglican.

The crisis has also called into question the role of the Lambeth Conference, a role which is highlighted by the one flaw in Nicolson's analysis. Resolution I.10, which declared homosexual practice to be "incompatible with Scriptures," and that same sex unions or ordaining those involved in same gender unions could not be sanctioned, did not constitute, as Nicolson suggests, an "agreement" among the provinces. That fact points to a feature of Anglicanism which is at once its bane and blessing—the autonomy of provinces and the concomitant absence of any centralized authority. The Lambeth Conference, as envisioned by Charles Thomas Longley, the Archbishop of Canterbury who convened the first Conference in 1867, was never intended to be legislative.[261] Lambeth resolutions, although they may well represent the thinking of the majority of the world's Anglican bishops, are hortatory. One theologian observes, for example, that for the Windsor Report to claim that a Lambeth resolution represents "the standard of Anglican teaching" is a bogus claim "because Lambeth has only an advisory role at best."[262]

The Church in the Province of Southern Africa has found itself embroiled in the debate over the Lambeth resolution. By and large, the bishops who voted in favor of the resolution came from provinces in developing countries. Most of the 115 bishops who voted against the resolution (of some 750 bishops in attendance) came from provinces in developed nations, such as the United States, Canada and Australia. The majority of the bishops from the CPSA, however, voted against the resolution. Moreover, the Primate of the CPSA joined the Primates of Brazil, Canada, Central Africa, Ireland, New Zealand, Scotland and Wales, and more than 150 other bishops who signed a statement addressed to gays and lesbians which apologized "for any sense of rejection" caused by the vote, and vowed to listen to homosexuals and "reflect with you theologically and spiritually on your lives and ministries."[263]

Since Lambeth, Archbishop Ndungane has issued a variety of statements both defending his position at Lambeth, and in 2003, defending the election of Bishop Gene Robinson in the Diocese of New Hampshire. Such statements, as we shall see, have resulted in strained relationships between Ndungane and his brother bishops on the continent of Africa, while at the same time have forged closer bonds between him and many of his counterparts in the West. Similarly, new alliances have been formed between the traditionalist minority in the United States and the African provinces other than South Africa. This is why I believe the issue of homosexuality to be an iconic one in Anglicanism today. There are many issues such as the authority of Scripture and the question of jurisdiction, and the nature of *episcope,* for example, which must be addressed. Yet homosexuality has become the unquestioned litmus test. It is the issue that is emblematic of the current divisions in Anglicanism. The position that a church holds on the subject is often understood to be a determinant of its biblical morality and ultimate orthodoxy.[264] Before looking at these developments, however, we should take a closer look on the workings of Lambeth and South Africa's pivotal role in it.

What Happened to the "Lambeth Principle"?

Although the Lambeth Conference came into being for the express purpose of settling differences among provinces, it has often achieved this end by devising ways for the provinces to "agree to disagree," rather than by arriving at a decision with which all member provinces are expected to concur. This method is called the "Lambeth Principle," and is also sometimes known as "reception." Through it, the Lambeth Conference consciously creates a way for provinces to opt for different courses of action while demonstrating mutual respect. The principle has been used most frequently when Lambeth has been faced with controversial issues, such as the ordination of women. In that instance, there was an agreement that if Province A ordains women and Province B does not, Province B recognizes Province A's right to ordain women, and Province A does not condemn Province B for not doing so. Sometimes the principle is observed through a period of discernment . . . during which "provinces will try to maintain the fullest communion possible even when some churches fail to accept or remain uncertain about the changes." [265]

Such an approach was attempted at the 1998 Lambeth Conference. As Convener of the Lambeth Section I, "Called to Full Humanity," Archbishop Ndungane prepared a study document, and distributed it to all bishops prior to the Conference. It stated: "The suggestion here is that approaching divisive issues of human sexuality from a way . . . [which] might also allow Christians to be pastorally sensitive to those with whom they disagree."[266] The subsection on human sexuality was, it should be noted, chaired by the Bishop of Johannesburg, the Right Reverend Duncan Buchanan. The deliberations were guided by the "Lambeth Principle," and the committee recommended a "reception" approach as regards the question of the ordination of homosexual persons, which would have provided an element of freedom that had found its way into resolutions on certain other issues in the past. This proposal was to have been "commended" to the Conference. The report, however, underwent revision at the hands of several conservative, "evangelical" bishops. Moreover, Archbishop Carey arguably swayed the vote by his statement that the amended resolution was reflective of "traditional Anglican orthodoxy."[267]

I would like to suggest that there are three major reasons why the Lambeth bishops did not apply the "Lambeth Principle" to the topic of homosexuality—specific Scriptural prohibition; cultural differences; and the residual effects of the history of mission. These factors, I think, provide us with a useful framework to better understand the issues before us.

Bishop Russell Looks at Scriptural Proscriptions

As is well known, there are passages of Scripture in both the Old and New Testaments which appear to condemn homosexual practice. Those passages are generally held to be the creation story in the first and second chapters of Genesis; the Sodom and Gomorrah story in Genesis 19:1–9; the Holiness Code proscriptions in Leviticus 18:22 and 20:13; and finally certain pericopes from Paul's epistles, viz., Romans 1:26–27; 1 Corinthians 6:9 and 1 Timothy 1–10. Because these texts seem to place homosexual activity outside the realm of acceptable moral behavior for the Christian, they form what Peter Gomes calls, "the religious basis for the prejudice against homosexuality often expressed by people of religious conviction."[268]

In *The Bible and Homosexuality,* his thoughtful book on the subject, David Russell, former Bishop of Grahamstown, does not begin, as some might have expected, grappling with and exegeting these texts. Rather, he begins by telling an African story from the Bible, the conversion of the Ethiopian eunuch. The eunuch's question, "How can I understand unless someone explains it to me?" (Acts 8:31) makes it clear that Holy Scripture, the fundamental text of our faith which also provides guidance for our daily life, *needs nevertheless to be interpreted "by the Church, by us, under the guidance of the Spirit."*[269]

Russell's readers resonate even more closely to contemporary issues which the bishop introduces, such as slavery, the role of women in the church, and remarriage after divorce. What these have in common is that there are Scriptural passages which appear to make unambiguous statements about them.[270] Russell then argues that since "there can surely therefore be no question but that the Church has indeed come to very different understandings concerning the meaning and 'authority for us' of certain texts . . . why then the heavy selective emphasis on the injunction against homosexual behavior?"[271] Russell then warns against biblical literalism. He describes as a "travesty" the fact that "the Bible has been tragically and dogmatically misused and abused down the ages to justify all manner of injustice and wrong," notably the subjugation of black people through slavery and apartheid, and the oppression of women. He points out, too, that the church, as regards these and other issues, "comes to new understanding about the meaning and requirements of Scripture, and that there is nothing wrong when the church often changes its mind."[272]

The genius of Russell's argument is that he ties the South African experience to an Anglican understanding of how Holy Scriptures have traditionally been interpreted. He cites a report of the Doctrine Commission of the Church of England on this topic which asserts that the church's task is "to consider how far these differences between scriptural times and our own affect the interpretation of the biblical message." In this regard, according to the report, "Christians need to discern what are the anchor points of their tradition, and what can be rethought in changing circumstances."[273] As Russell expressed it at the CPSA Synod, "In approaching Scripture in our mainstream Anglican tradition, we distinguish between those things which were of the times, and those which are for all times."[274]

The idea that Bishop Russell's approach to the Bible might lead to an acceptance of homosexual behavior under some circumstances is still unacceptable to the vast majority of his fellow African bishops who understand Scripture differently. At the last Lambeth Conference, for example, Bishop Peter Adebiyi of Nigeria said that to ignore the biblical condemnation of homosexuality and to recognize such behavior as acceptable, would be to commit "evangelical suicide." The Bishop of Mityana, Uganda, asserted that Anglicans in his region were aware of what science and philosophy have to say about homosexuality, but declared that for them, "the final truth resides in Scripture."[275]

It is imperative that we understand the significance of this development in another context. Such an approach to Holy Scripture bears little or no resemblance to the Anglican method of biblical interpretation described by Bishop Russell. Indeed, the Lambeth resolution "seeks to abandon more traditional Anglican principles for using and interpreting the Bible in favor of a hermeneutic that insists that the Bible is to be interpreted 'on its own terms.'"[276] Indeed, one of the proposed resolutions, introduced by the bishops of the Province of Central Africa, cited in the Appendix and commended to the Primates, would have committed the Conference to belief in "the primary authority of the Scriptures, according to their own testimony, as supported by our own historical tradition." The resolution pointedly continues: "The Scripture's revelation of Jesus the Christ must continue to illuminate, challenge and transform cultures, structures, systems and ways of thinking, especially those secular views that predominate in our society today."

Supremacy of Scripture?

In light of these facts, it is clear that the principal reason for the impasse in the Anglican Communion today over the matter of human sexuality is how Anglicans make use of the Bible. But it is more than a difference of textual interpretation. It is, more significantly, a basic disagreement over the role of the Bible itself among Anglicans. The phrase "primary authority of Scriptures" in the resolution cited above is arguably a particularly un-Anglican phrase. It smacks of the *sola Scriptura* teaching espoused by the Reformers, which Anglicans explicitly rejected in favor of an appeal to tradition and reason, as well as Scripture. It must be remembered that "Richard Hooker helped shape future Anglican thinking by his insistence that while the fundamental truths of the Christian faith are obvious even to the unlearned, the Bible as a whole is not self-evident [but] requires the use of 'theological reason.'"[277]

I was able to witness an expression of such a belief at the "Hope and a Future" conference, convened by the Network of Anglican Dioceses and Parishes, an organization that believes that the Episcopal Church, through the consecration of a non-celibate gay man as bishop, has erred and has overturned two thousand years of biblical teaching. When asked if he would remain supportive of the Network's goals, Peter Jasper Akinola, Archbishop of Nigeria, the largest province in Anglicanism, held his Bible over his head and declared that he is "in communion with all of those who uphold the Bible as the Word of God, and who are freed of structures [in his opinion, such as the American and Canadian churches] which deny the *supremacy* of the Word of God. As long as we hold together with the Bible," he concluded, "we are with you every inch of the way."[278] There is more than a suggestion here that the new conservative forces believe that they are faithful to Scripture, and have, by virtue of that faithfulness, an exclusive claim on it, a claim that they would say other Anglicans have forfeited by virtue of their apostate actions. When seen in light of this "Bible against the world" approach, we can grasp the depth of the rift between factions on the matter of human sexuality.

The belief in the inerrancy and supremacy of Scripture has brought about another serious consequence, namely that such an attitude shuts off debate and forestalls any possibility of further discussion among member churches of the Anglican Communion. The effect of this development is that it renders impossible the honoring of the Lambeth resolution which mandated dialogue with homosexual persons so that the Communion could become more informed about homosexuality. Not surprisingly, several primates have ignored that mandate with impunity, and have justified their positions by pointing to the "plain words" of Scripture. Henry Luke Orombi, for example, Archbishop of Uganda, has ruled out debate, demanding that homosexual persons must either repent of their behavior or go their way: "I do not think there is a debate. When God gives his word, you either take it or leave it. . . . The Bible defines marriage as between one man and one woman. The Episcopal Church of America hasn't followed the biblical teachings on sexuality and that's why we're against them."[279]

Such rigid views point to yet another and more serious consequence of this novel approach to Anglican biblical theology, namely that holding of "unorthodox" views on the question of human sexuality has been used to justify the virtual exclusion of whole provinces from the Anglican fellowship. This has been described by one American theologian as "the greatest irony," because the much touted theological diversity so evident at Lambeth "should have as its touchstone a point of view that would curtail or eliminate diversity in favor of a more simplistic, authoritarian use of Scripture." This only violates both the principle of diversity (on which catholicity depends) as well as the principle of charity.[280] But perhaps the strongest condemnation of this latter-day un-Anglican development within the bosom of Anglicanism was

expressed by Khotso Makhulu, Archbishop of Central Africa and senior primate of the Anglican Communion, in the closing sermon at Lambeth XIII.
Decrying what he referred to as "tyrants using the Bible as armor," he declared
that he would never tolerate tyranny "from those who claim the love of the
Bible over everyone else." Expressing a fear that following this theological
course of action would "inexorably lead us to intolerance," Makhulu made it
abundantly clear that such a use and understanding of Scripture were contrary
and inimical to the Anglican ethos. He concluded his sermon by saying, "I
pray to God that the spirit of Anglicanism will survive, that we shall come to
engage each other and find the best foot forward."[281]

How Cultural Differences Affect 'Truths' about Sexuality

The South African theologian Paul Germond makes the observation that
Presiding Bishop Frank Griswold, former primate of the Episcopal Church
USA, lives in a culture "steeped in a commitment to individual human rights,
which is seen as a central expression of the Christian gospel." Diversity and
freedom of conscience are understood to be unalienable rights; clergy and
laypersons who are openly gay are active in the life of the church; and one of
the articulated roles of the church is to be a place of refuge for marginalized
groups.[282] Indeed, in response to the Windsor Report, Bishop Griswold wrote:
"It is important to note here that in the Episcopal Church we are seeking
to live the gospel in a society where homosexuality is openly discussed and
increasingly acknowledged in all areas of our public life."[283] Germond's
comment is quite accurate in his assessment of American culture. What may
well be added is that the Episcopal Church, which has had a unique, symbiotic
relationship with the American Republic since they both came into being at
the end of the eighteenth century, probably best reflects the mores of the
society known for its veneration of the principle of rugged individualism. Self-
expression or "doing one's own thing" is seen as an unalienable, God-given
right. The Episcopal Church's attitudes toward African Americans, women
and gays within the last two generations, while the fruit of much theological
debate, are nonetheless reflective of attitudinal shifts in the society in the areas
of civil, women's and gay rights.

In Africa, conversely, there is still in the culture a reverence for
community. The default position of the African is more likely to be a concern

for what is good for the family or tribe or village, as opposed to the individual. Therefore, an English priest-theologian who exercised most of his ministry in Uganda can rightly observe that "personal issues of sexuality, whether heterosexual or homosexual, have not been debated with such openness."[284] Ndungane concurs, observing that there exists in South Africa not only a blind spot about homosexuality, but sexuality in general. "Africa's complex cultural history means there is still much to learn across the spectrum of human sexuality—in relationships between men and women also." He points out, for example, that South African marriage customs perpetuate the inequality of women and fall far short of biblical standards.[285] Iterating this point in relationship to homosexuality in particular, he commented, "We in Africa need to learn more about our sexuality. . . . I know people who are gay and lesbian and who are African. The issue of orientation knows no culture and my fellow bishops are in denial."[286] Such a view was replicated in the remarks of other South Africans with whom I spoke. Canon Luke Pato, for example, said that many South Africans deny the fact of homosexuality, believing in some cases that it is "a white thing, and not an African thing." Yet he pointed out that families are breaking up "because of something that doesn't exist." Germond believes that the fault lines running through the Anglican Communion are still largely beneath the surface in South Africa, but would surface in the near future.

Germond also states that Africans' theologies of sexuality are also affected by the "radically different contexts in which Anglicans live." He mentions, for example, that Archbishop Peter Akinola of Nigeria must provide leadership for a province in which Christians often clash with Muslims, who staunchly oppose homosexuality. Akinola believes, therefore, that his challenge is to refute, by word and example, accusations that Anglicans are part and parcel of the moral decay of the Western world. As a consultant to the Lambeth bishops observed, "Many bishops from Africa . . . felt it hugely important to obtain a clear condemnation of homosexual practice, not so much for their own pastoral needs, but so that they would not be the object of scorn by dominant Muslim populations."[287]

The radically disparate contexts in which Anglicans do their respective ministries must be acknowledged as a challenge to communication about all issues, especially human sexuality. Within the past generation, attitudes toward homosexuality in industrialized nations have changed dramatically.

While there is hardly universal acceptance, there have been steady, perceptible inroads. Every major religious body is grappling with the extent to which homosexuality is tolerated, and the extent to which homosexual persons, and couples, are accepted. Most Africans, on the other hand, often understand such developments "as a movement away from Scripturally based moral principles to an ethic based entirely of individuals and their sexual satisfaction."[288] Michael Peers, the late Primate of the Canadian Church, addressed the dilemma. He admitted that most Anglicans who go to church on Sunday are Africans who "have very different views on this subject than Canadians do." He went on to affirm, however, the positive contributions of gays and lesbians, concluding, "That is where we stand, and I can't believe that we are going to move from there."[289]

Human Sexuality and the History of Mission

One factor which has greatly contributed to the entrenched positions held by opposing sides of the sexuality debate is historical. Anglican missionary activity that flourished during the Victorian era was not only religious in nature. It had a clear and unabashed social agenda as well. Seldom was a house of worship erected in any outpost of the Empire without a school in its shadow. As often as not, there was a hospital as well. The British, believing their society to be the quintessential model of civilization, "sought to re-structure local society according to what it understood to be Christian norms and values."[290] As it was impossible for the English psyche to understand Christianity apart from its English context, this meant that the missionary enterprise was also, by default, a cultural indoctrination.[291] "Christian" names were given in baptism and traditional initiation rites were often suppressed entirely. Native instruments were banned in worship. In short, indigenization was not the order of the day.

Such attitudes and practices affected sexual relations, which "were scrutinized in the light of the missionaries' espoused morality,"[292] a morality informed by the repressive practices of Victorian England, where it was considered improper even for the legs of tables to be exposed and uncovered. "One of the marks of the early converts was their acceptance of a strictly controlled sexuality and the adoption of monogamy, celebrated by a church wedding."[293] Since conformity to the monogamous standard was seen as a way that converts were set apart from the rest of society, sexual relations before or outside of marriage were forbidden, polygamy was not countenanced, and divorced persons were scorned. Women, who in some African societies had had prominent leadership roles, often gave these up in order to conform to the values held dear by gentlewomen in the Church of England. Needless to say, homosexual behavior, if it ever surfaced, would be roundly condemned, not only because it was seen as immoral or unbiblical, but because the practice could not be reconciled with the societal expectation that individuals should marry and have children. There is anecdotal evidence that at Lambeth XIII, some African bishops expressed incredulity at Western bishops' intolerance of their "conservative" stands, since the African bishops believed that they were doing nothing more than exhibiting the moral standards brought to them by Western missionaries in the first place.

There is another aspect of this phenomenon. The third-world objections do not derive solely from different interpretations of Scripture or dissimilar cultural situations. The tension can also be traced to an historical tension between the Western missionary churches and the African missionized churches.[294] Akinola, in commenting on the decision of the American church to ordain a gay man as bishop, asked, "Do we not see here a new imperialism?"[295] After General Convention's confirmation of the election of that bishop, the Archbishop of South East Asia declared that "this act cannot but be seen as arrogant, with total disregard and contempt for the sacramental unity of the Communion."[296] The Archbishop of Uganda, after the consecration, pointedly remarked: "We grieve because we remember the pain that has come from similar *imperial* actions in the past."[297]

Such statements, according to Willis Jenkins, an Episcopal Church missionary appointee in Uganda, indicate that there were unresolved issues between ECUSA and the African churches long before the Minneapolis Convention. Although its actions are not now expressed with the same self-righteous disdain as a Victorian missionary hymn, ECUSA, nevertheless, "had not sustained Incarnational and missional concern for real and rooted differences in the ecclesial life and pastoral care among Anglican provinces."[298] Understandably, then, many Africans respond with resentment to a church whose byword is "diversity" but which often fails to honor such diversity when it takes the form of different attitudes toward sexual orientation and behavior. In many ways, the debate on homosexuality has exposed the cultural intransigence of the member churches of the Anglican Communion.

Lambeth XIII has been described as the first postmodern Lambeth Conference precisely because it became clear that it had no identifiable center.[299] Moreover, as we have observed, Lambeth XIII virtually jettisoned Anglicanism's time-honored hermeneutical approach to Scripture. There was also evidence at Lambeth that western churches were loath to give up the power they traditionally wielded, predicated on their wealth and influence, while the new African churches were eager to bask in their newfound power based on sheer numbers. The debate on sexuality, more than any other, forced the Communion to ask if it is possible for churches that do not respect each other's views to coexist under the Anglican umbrella. The Communion that has long prided itself for maintaining unity in its diversity is discovering that there is a cost and a strain associated with that Herculean task.

The South African Response: "The New Apartheid"?
South African Theologians

All of the South Africans whom I interviewed made comments which suggested that the peculiar history of the nation has played a distinctive role on the understanding of homosexuality in both church and society. Those views, by and large, stand in stark contrast to the prevailing views on the topic on the rest of the African continent. While emphasizing that there is "a full spectrum of views on virtually every issue," Bishop Nuttall indicated that tolerance of homosexuality is an example of the fact that "our strength has been in our ability to hold on to one another despite differences. We have learned to do so based on our experiences as a nation and a church."[300] Similarly, Desmond Tutu explained that the CPSA's ability to deal with the issue of homosexuality was honed in the struggle against apartheid and the debate over the ordination of women.[301]

What these comments have in common is that they recognize the struggles of gays and lesbians as a human rights issue. It is no coincidence that the question of human sexuality at the 1998 Lambeth Conference was considered under Section I, entitled "Called to full humanity."[302] In addition to the church's attitude toward homosexual persons, that section also dealt with such populations as displaced persons, women and children, victims of war and persons suffering from the effects of persecution in such places as Rwanda and the Sudan. The implication is clear. Lambeth XIII, which could have arguably considered the topic under "Called to be faithful in a plural world," chose instead to make a statement that like the homeless, the survivors of genocide, women and children, and those most adversely affected by the burden of international debt, homosexual persons have been denied their full humanity—and to deny fellow human beings of their very humanity is tantamount to abandoning the baptismal vow to "strive for justice and peace among all people and respect the dignity of every human being."[303] Nor was the choice of Archbishop Ndungane to chair the section a coincidence. He was named to that post because his experiences in South Africa made him especially suitable for the task. An "alumnus" of Robben Island, he was on the front lines in the battle against apartheid; as a bishop and theologian he had helped the church wrestle with women's ordination and its response to the AIDS crisis.

Professor Jonathan Draper observed that in South Africa, the human rights clauses of the Constitution, which provide protection for all persons, including gays, are fiercely defended. "The ethos of South Africa is different than other African nations," he commented. "Because the law here tends to protect human rights, the church is disposed to do likewise. In countries where there is no such Constitution or law, e.g., Nigeria or Uganda, the church tends to be more doctrinaire, hard-line, and resistant to the protection of rights, e.g., of women or gays."[304] This would suggest that the church's ability and willingness to be a prophetic voice depends in large measure on the society in which it finds itself. In a similar vein, Archbishop Ndungane observed that the Anglican Church has held together despite huge diversities—in race, ecclesiology, theology, culture, language, as well as an intensely divisive political system.[305] Ndungane also believes that the extent to which the Synod of the CPSA has expressed a tolerance for, and in some cases an acceptance of homosexuality is a direct consequence of the fact that the South African Constitution is founded on nondiscrimination.[306]

When asked about why he thought there was more acceptance of homosexuality in the CPSA than in other provinces, Thabo Makgoba, Bishop of Grahamstown, stated that tolerance has grown out of a strong sense of democracy. He added that "unlike African countries in other provinces who made the transition from colony to independent state by mere transference— the lowering of the Union Jack and the hoisting of the new national flag—our theology has been shaped by our past." Another contrast he mentioned was that in South Africa, Christians in general and Anglicans in particular (he reminded me that South Africa is Africa's oldest province) are not intimidated by other faiths. South Africans are accustomed to living "cheek to jowl" with those of other faith traditions, such as Roman Catholic, Muslim and Jewish. Bishop Thabo saw this as contrasting with other nations where Islam is a threat, dominating the religious scene. He concluded by saying, "In South Africa, our colonizers have made us question things. Our contextual situation has helped to form our ecclesiology."[307]

These comments all suggest that the struggle against apartheid and the reverence for democracy and freedom as expressed in South Africa's Constitution have created an atmosphere in which the question of homosexuality, to the South African mind, is inextricably linked with the issue of justice, a fact which places the South African church more in sympathy with the majority of North American Anglicanism. This means, too, that the South African stance is in stark contrast to the fact that elsewhere on the continent of Africa, homosexuality is viewed, both in church and society, as a matter linked almost solely to biblical morality. It is for this reason, according to the Reverend Janet Trisk, a lecturer at the College of the Transfiguration, that many Africans actually question Archbishop Ndungane's right to be called an African![308]

Dean Edward King

The connection between homosexuality and justice is not a new, post-apartheid phenomenon. Edward King, who was appointed dean of St. George's Cathedral, Cape Town, by Archbishop deBlank in 1958, and served for thirty years under five archbishops, made these remarks in a speech to students at the University of Cape Town in 1983, a year which, in terms of the debate over human sexuality, is reckoned as ancient history.

> It is the quality of love, and not whether people are homosexual or heterosexual, that matters in sexual relationships. While heterosexual relationships and marriage are the normative path set by God for most people, alongside that has to be an acceptance of homosexual relationships. I would not see homosexual relationships as perfect, but they are natural for the people involved in them, in that it is their true nature. Some same-sex relationships

are better than their heterosexual counterparts, and, because of the quality of love, I am sure they make God happier. While I would not marry two homosexuals, if there were two men or two women who were committed to a long-term relationship together, I would be prepared to give them a blessing and prayers in church.[309]

To understand the comment in context, it might be helpful to understand something of Dean King's ministry at the Cathedral. The strategic location of the Cathedral, in the heart of downtown, surrounded by seats of government and banking houses, meant that it was, during his deanship, often a place for "prayerful protest." For this and other reasons, he was extremely popular among students. Sometimes, these demonstrations became violent, as police violated the sanctuary of that holy space with clubs and tear gas! There were, predictably, many who did not like what the Cathedral stood for. But they came to understand that, in the catholic tradition now a hallmark of the province, "religion and life were not separate entities, but, as in scripture, indivisible."[310] When he provided tents on the cathedral grounds for evicted squatters in 1977, he said to his detractors, "It is quite hopeless to sing hymns of social importance on Sunday, and do nothing of social consequence on Monday."[311] His theology of the church was summed up in a speech he made at Cape Town City Hall: "If the church is not concerned with freedom, education, justice and dignity, then it is concerned with irrelevancies and peripheral frivolities." The Cathedral was, to its dean, as St. George's guide book proclaimed, "a symbol of unity in diversity, a temple of dialogue, a broadcasting station for the voice of the poor, a tower of reconciliation, and a motel for pilgrims."

It is not surprising, therefore, that Dean King approached moral problems not as questions of abstract debate, but as questions about individuals trying to live with integrity.[312] Thus, it can be said that he was concerned more about homosexuals than about homosexuality. He brought to the matter first and foremost the concern of a pastor, not that of a moral or biblical theologian. But he did not dismiss biblical arguments claiming homosexual behavior to be sinful. He merely raised the question as to whether those passages needed to be reconsidered in light of modern scholarship. To Dean King, homosexual persons were another group whom church and society had marginalized. It seemed to him incongruous to fight for the rights of blacks in South Africa, and to ignore the plight of gays and lesbians.

Archbishop Tutu

The last archbishop under whom Dean King served was Desmond Tutu. Soon after he became primate, he told his fellow bishops that he was "unhappy" with the church's stance on the issue of homosexuality, and he urged them to wrestle with the matter. In his own wrestling with the issue, he saw it, like his colleagues, as a matter of justice.[313] "We say that celibacy is a vocation—that is, some are called to that state and some are not. And yet, those who maintain that homosexual acts are sinful are happy to impose celibacy on ten percent of the population! We also maintain that sexual activity between a husband and wife is crucial to their growth as a couple. It is an act in which each learns to give to the other in an attempt to be more godlike. If this is true of heterosexuals, why cannot it be true of homosexuals?"

Tutu's theology of justice is predicated on a simple sense of equity. Believing that all sexuality is a gift of God, he contends that it is impossible to be opposed to discrimination based on race or gender, while condoning discrimination based on sexual orientation. The common thread to Tutu is that race, gender and sexual orientation are things over which human beings have no control. Recently, in a foreword to a book published by Amnesty International entitled *Sex, Love and Homophobia: Lesbian, gay, bisexual and transgendered lives* (London, 2004) Tutu expanded on this theme. He declared homophobia to be "a crime against humanity, every bit as unjust as apartheid" because in each case people were being made to suffer for something they could do nothing about. Whereas most African bishops focus on what they understand to be the moral flaws of the homosexual person, Tutu concentrates on the moral flaws of those in church and society who mistreat homosexual persons. Tutu's approach challenges the righteous indignation of those who believe it justifiable to condemn homosexual persons with impunity. He asks those casting the stone to examine their own consciences and to ask why they believe such condemnatory behavior to be Christian.

In considering the issue, the Archbishop emeritus of Cape Town does not neglect to examine the matter from a biblical perspective, but he does so contextually. He is impatient with a "pick-and-choose" approach to Scripture, in which, for example, the church is willing "to dismiss the unequivocal Dominical words on divorce," while at the same time the church is willing to recognize the words of St. Paul on homosexuality as "utterances of unchanging truth." Part of Tutu's contextual approach enables him to ask questions having to do with Jesus' consistency. He believes Jesus is clear, for example, in his castigation of pride and hypocrisy; yet nowhere does Jesus bash the sexual sinner in such a way. In raising these questions, Tutu challenges those who would uphold the so-called "plain meaning of Scripture." Rather than proof-texting, Tutu's biblical theology demands that he look at texts in context, seeking truth from consistent themes and trajectories of teaching, rather than "evidence" based on isolated texts.

Tutu believes that "Christ must be weeping bitterly" that the world is spending so much time and energy on a preoccupation with the question of human sexuality, at a time when in some African countries whole generations are being wiped out by AIDS. Never opinionless, the archbishop proffered an explanation for this phenomenon: "When problems are intractable, it is human nature to go after the one straightforward issue. It makes people feel good. The stridency that both church and society have exhibited with respect to this issue should make us hold our heads in shame." In this comment, I believe, Tutu points to yet another reason why homosexuality has become an iconic issue in Anglicanism. It is a convenient issue to which people can devote a great deal of energy, even as they ignore other pressing challenges at their doorstep.

Archbishop Ndungane
The Flawed Methodology of Lambeth XIII

Tutu's successor inherited a church whose leaders showed a deep sensitivity to homosexual persons coupled with a commitment to address the matter with integrity. Long before Lambeth XIII mandated the Communion to do so, the CPSA has been in a listening process, learning from gay people in church and society. Archbishop Ndungane is not given to making categorical pronouncements like so many of his brother primates; his tendency is instead to look at the issues and to raise questions. In fact, in a recent article, he wrote: "In my own exploration of this topic [Scripture and how it relates to the question of homosexuality] the more I have delved into the questions, the less sure I feel about any of the answers. That, for me, is good theology."[314]

In an attempt to lay the groundwork for a theological discussion on the topic of homosexuality, Ndungane starts with Scripture, but he makes it clear that although the Bible "is regarded as a primary source for doing theology," it must be considered in conjunction with reason, faith, culture, experience and tradition. He regards as specious a method of theological inquiry into this or any topic in which Scripture is "used as a predominant standard over and against which the different positions in the debate were measured." It is noteworthy in light of the resolution on homosexuality passed at the 1998 Lambeth Conference which is almost entirely predicated on an appeal to the "supremacy of Scripture." Ndungane points out the irony that it was at the 1948 Conference that the assembled bishops concurred that secondary authority (primary authority being given to the Trinity) "is distributed interactively between a variety of elements including scripture, reason, tradition, the creeds, ministry, the witness of the saints and the *consensus fidelium*, thus excluding any one of these from claiming primary status." Ndungane sees this as evidence that Anglicanism has drifted far away from this theological moorings.

Ndungane essentially makes three observations about how he believes Scripture to have been misused in relation to the Lambeth resolution. First, he maintains that those who opposed homosexuality cited several biblical texts which at face value condemn the practice. But, he points out, the texts were not examined in their context; nor was the understanding of homosexuality in biblical times taken into consideration. In other words, it was assumed that the Bible spoke clearly on the issue, and that homosexuality is sinful. The archbishop sees this approach as being a way to "support a particular prejudice" since it sees the Bible as a document frozen in time, and refuses to be informed by "the advent and development of our current medical, psychological and sociological studies."

Second, Lambeth failed to look toward or rely upon sources other than the Bible for doing theology. In addition to refusing to be influenced or guided by insights from the sciences, the group charged with the responsibility of listening to the stories of homosexual persons refused to do so. The third issue is not unrelated. It is the decision of the Lambeth Conference to arrogate to itself the right to make pronouncements on the topic, including a directive about how homosexual persons are to be received, or not, into fellowship throughout the Anglican Communion. Those bishops, who were later quick to remonstrate against "arrogant" and "precipitous" actions on the part of the American and Canadian churches which allegedly contributed to the divisions in which Anglicanism now finds itself should ask themselves if they should take a beam out of their own eye. The bishops' actions, which Ndungane maintains "have highlighted divisions in the Communion," were no less disruptive to worldwide Anglicanism. The Primates, arguably emboldened by the bishops' actions, later issued directives on this topic, which they assumed would be binding for the whole Communion. This action, and the re-organization of the Anglican Consultative Council, making all primates *ex officio* members, have seriously shifted the balance of power which had previously existed, to the extent that many believe that Anglicanism is moving toward a curial structure of Anglican church governance.

Homosexuality and Justice

Like his predecessor, Ndungane sees homosexuality as a justice issue. According to Luke Pato, he is fully aware that South Africa and her churches will continue to play a leading role in the debate. Fully aware, however, that homosexuality is a sensitive issue, he has been cautious. His comments have been irenic, and he has asked those on different sides of the issue to approach it with charity and forbearance. He also encourages his audience to look at the issue in perspective. Believing that a preoccupation with personal feelings "will undermine our standing and ability to act in other areas of conflict," he reminds them that "our calling to bring good news to the poor, in a world where half the population live in poverty, must not be jeopardized." Before the Lambeth Commission met to make recommendations about how the Communion would go forward in the wake of the developments in North America, Ndungane said that his "prayer is that God will lead them into creative solutions that will help heal not just our own pains, but the pains of the broken and hurting world in which we live."[315]

Ndungane, despite his prominent place on the world's stage, never forgets his role as shepherd to the people of his province, in which capacity he is both teacher and pastor. While many of his African counterparts make categorical pronouncements about homosexuality, with little or no pastoral concern expressed for homosexual persons, Ndungane has been quick to point out the painful cost of the ongoing debate, not only to homosexual persons themselves but to the combatants on both sides. At a recent General Synod of the Province, he said it was time for Anglicans to urgently address the issue in a manner that will generate mutual understanding and bring people out of their "corners of conviction." He has also noted the "pastoral needs" of gay and lesbian persons, and has expressed gratitude for their contributions to the life of the province. He has also invited them to participate in diocesan task forces which would look into ways that gays would be "affirmed and welcomed" in the church.

Homosexuality a "Smokescreen"?

In reading the writings and sermons of Njongonkulu Ndungane, one is struck by his frequent use of the phrase "Gospel imperative." To him, the Gospel imperative is the means through which "Christians must learn better ways of working through difference and diversity, in order to refine, enrich and strengthen the Church in its vocation to follow Christ and forward God's mission in the world."[316] In a sermon preached at the Convention of the Diocese of Washington, he described the Gospel imperative as that which "urges us to hold together as we work through disagreements. We must face the challenge to develop an ethic of together-in-difference."[317]

Remarkably, in that same sermon, Ndungane makes it clear that "homo-sexuality is not the issue at stake." He believes it to be an issue which is em-blematic of, or even a smokescreen for "a far more important principle which the political struggles of today's globalizing world are echoing." He identifies it as "the question of whether one world view, one political perspective, one theological stance, overrules, is right, can assert dominance, and render all other standpoints inferior and illegitimate." The alternative, to Ndungane, is that "none of us has the monopoly on knowledge and understanding; our lives are enriched and our horizons expanded when we encounter other, authentic expressions of human life, culture and spirituality."[318]

In raising such a question, the Archbishop of Cape Town assumes the role of the little boy in "The Emperor's New Clothes." That child, unafraid of causing offense and in danger of losing no court sinecure, could unabashedly proclaim that the monarch, whose sycophantic and mendacious tailors had convinced him that he was arrayed in the finest silks, was in fact quite naked. While not a few, mostly conservative theologians have accused the church of wedding the spirit of the age and falling victim to relativism,[319] Ndungane has exposed the nakedness of the church in a different sphere, namely that it has begun to walk in lockstep with a global ideology that disparages diversity and even eschews individual freedom.

If Ndungane is right, it means that a doctrinaire, fundamentalist and often judgmental theological stance has emerged as the handmaid to oppressive political systems wherever they exist. This is why Archbishop Ndungane's theology, into which is woven a deep concern for victims of crushing poverty, people living with AIDS, those who have been displaced by political upheaval, as well as homosexual persons, is of a whole cloth. This is why the Gospel imperative is so important to him, because he hopes that it will keep the church focused on the broader picture of suffering and not the narrow moral issue of sexuality. This, indeed, is why he places great emphasis on the autonomy of Anglican provinces. It is not because he believes each province must be sovereign, answerable only to itself. Rather, he believes that because we have never been a communion "based around a single statement of faith or set of rules . . . but a church that has held together through a shared past of deep historical roots," the Anglican Communion is uniquely qualified to be a model for true *koinonia*.

Njongonkulu Winston Hugh Ndungane has demonstrated that the raging debate over human sexuality in general, and homosexuality in particular, has become a symbol for the struggle for its identity that Anglicanism faces today.

Chapter VIII

"There Is Always Something New Coming out of Africa"
South Africa as the Crucible of the Communion

Our experience is something we can offer to the global Communion for their enrichment. Indeed, there is more hope we can share. Our Province is a microcosm of the whole Communion, and of today's global world—we are almost a microcosm of heaven, where Revelation speaks of every race and nation and language and tongue being present! No other Province has the same breadth of diversity. Here anyone and everyone is welcome, and fully one of us. Our ability to live united in our diversity is a very special gift. Let us not become so focused on differences that we fail to see what riches we share. Let us go forward in hope together, and offer our life to the Communion, and indeed, to the worldwide church, as a beacon of hope into the shared future of the whole Christian family.

— The Most Revd Njongonkulu Ndungane, Archbishop of Cape Town
In his charge to the 31st Provincial Synod of the CPSA, July 2005

Parallels Between Lambeth I and Lambeth XIV

The agenda for Lambeth XIV in 2008 may well include items not un-like those with which the first Lambeth wrestled. The issue of the authority of Scripture loomed large in 1867 because Colenso's biblical theology was deemed heretical. At Lambeth XIV, traditionalist Anglicans will doubtless maintain that their progressive counterparts have jettisoned two thousand years of biblical teaching on sexual morality and the sacrament of matrimony. The question of the authority and jurisdiction of bishops can be seen as another "great gulf fixed" between liberal and conservative factions then and now. At the first Lambeth, the question was not only the obvious problem of two bishops claiming authority in an overlapping jurisdiction; the greater issue was whether Robert Gray could properly claim archiepiscopal and metropolitical authority over another bishop in South Africa. The Privy Council ruled that he could not. The understanding of what constitutes a diocese and what constitutes a province was an issue that had to be addressed by the seventy-six bishops who met at Lambeth Palace in 1867, and it will be high on the agenda of the bishops who meet at the University of Kent in 2008. The former group had to grapple with whether the sees of Natal and Maritzburg could coexist in virtually the same place.

The mitered leaders of the church at the beginning of the third millennium will have to grapple with the thornier issue of whether a diocese (or a province) must be geographical at all. Lines between ecclesiastical jurisdictions are held by many today to be porous. Already, as in the case of the Network of Anglican Dioceses and Parishes, alliances are being forged among dispersed communities who claim not geographical proximity but a theological and ideological kindred spirit. Too, many parishes in the Episcopal Church have, along such lines, affiliated with dioceses in Africa and South America. The Province of Nigeria has consecrated an American priest to serve as a bishop to orthodox Nigerians and others in the United States, and several parishes, notably in the Diocese of Virginia, have voted to sever their ties with the Episcopal Church and swear allegiance instead to the Church in Nigeria.

The larger question of who is in communion with whom, therefore, is not a new phenomenon in Anglicanism. The bishops of Maritzburg and Natal did not recognize each other because the South African church had excommunicated Colenso on the grounds of heresy. Today, some Global South provinces have declared the Episcopal Church USA and the Anglican Church of Canada to have removed themselves from the Anglican fold because of their recent decisions having to do with human sexuality. Whether these actions are grounds for such separation are issues which the Lambeth XIV bishops will not be able to avoid. The knotty issue of who, in the light of such disputes, has a right to church property is a matter which was taken up by the Privy Council in the wake of Colenso's trial, and it is a matter which Anglican bodies or ecclesiastical and civil courts will have to make decisions about in the wake of anticipated schisms within Anglicanism today.

Another commonality that binds Lambeth I and Lambeth XIV is a perception that the whole Communion is wounded by the acts of one province, even one diocese. This was essentially what was contended by the Canadian bishops who implored Archbishop Longley to convene Lambeth I; it is certainly a charge that has been on the lips of many of Anglicanism's greater and lesser prelates in recent years, and will be at the heart of Lambeth's 2008 deliberations.

The Challenges of a Post-Windsor Anglicanism

The consecration of an openly gay bishop in the Diocese of New Hampshire (USA) and the approval of a rite for same-sex blessings in the Diocese of New Westminster (Canada)[320] have proved to be serious blows to the already fragile unity of the Anglican Communion. In the wake of these unprecedented actions, the Archbishop of Canterbury called an extraordinary meeting of the Primates of the Anglican Communion, which took place at Lambeth Palace in October 2003, and subsequently named a commission under the chairmanship of the Archbishop of Armagh, which has since promulgated the Lambeth Report on Communion, commonly known as the Windsor Report. In an attempt to achieve what has been called a realignment of Anglicanism, the report made several far-reaching recommendations through which the ethos, polity and governance of Anglicanism were drastically recast.

Each of the report's recommendations chips away at the autonomy which the Provinces of the Communion have traditionally enjoyed, and replaces it with some aspect of a centralized authority. For example, the Archbishop of Canterbury is now expected to be more than a "figurehead," but to "articulate the mind of the Communion" and to "speak directly to any provincial situation on behalf of the Communion," and that such intervention would not be deemed to be outside interference. Moreover, the authors of the report made it clear that it is within the power of the archbishop to invite or not invite to the Primates' Meeting and the Lambeth Conference whomsoever he pleases

[Paragraphs 108–110 of the Windsor Report]. The report also made provision for a Council of Advice to provide support to the archbishop when such decisions are made [111–112]. To help ensure that all member provinces would be singing from the same hymnal, so to speak, an Anglican Covenant [117–120] would bind each province to "the acknowledgment of a common identity" and provide for the management of Communion affairs, including disputes.

While the relevance of these provisions to the Episcopal Church can readily be seen, Windsor went on to make specific demands of the American branch of Anglicanism. The Episcopal Church was asked to "express regret" for the pain its actions had caused other members of the Communion, and to effect a moratorium on elections to the episcopate of others in same-sex relationships [134]. In a recommendation aimed in particular at the Anglican Church of Canada, Windsor requested that bishops not authorize rites for same-sex blessings, and that those who have done so express regret [143–145].

In June 2004, the Anglican Consultative Council, at its 13th meeting held in Nottingham, England, voted to suspend the Anglican Church of Canada and the Episcopal Church (USA) from its deliberations until the 2008 Lambeth Conference—although strictly speaking, the Council voted, by a narrow margin, to accept the voluntary withdrawal of those two churches as requested by the Primates at their second special meeting, held in Dromantine, Ireland in February 2005.[321] Given these unprecedented events in the life of the church since the last Lambeth Conference, the bishops at the 2008 Lambeth Conference, meeting as a body for the first time since these developments, will have a lot on their plate. Americans and Canadians were allowed to be present at the ACC as observers, however, and it was on that occasion that the American representatives presented their response to Windsor, entitled "To Set Our Hope on Christ," which outlines the theological struggles around issues of human sexuality with which the Episcopal Church has grappled for forty years. It described how the Episcopal Church had "come to support the blessing of [same-sex] unions and the ordination and consecration of persons in those unions."[322]

"The Truth Newly Perceived?"

These and other recent developments in the Anglican world have set a mise-en-scene that is remarkably similar to that of Anglicanism in the mid-nineteenth century. An historian's description of the climate of Anglicanism at the time of Colenso's trial can be applied in almost every respect to the situation in which Ecclesia Anglicana now finds itself:

> The age was . . . an age of litigation and controversy. . . . The reason for all this litigious bitterness in the Church of England is ultimately to be traced to the fact that at this time all theology was in the melting pot. To some it seemed that the age-old, accepted truths were suddenly being treated as of no account. To others it seemed that the truth was being compelled to wear a strait-jacket of conventional theology. It is not surprising that men fought as hard as they could, some to maintain the faith once delivered to the saints, others for the right to preach the truth newly perceived. To some it was imperative that the mouths of wickedness be stopped; to others equally imperative that the truth be published at whatever cost. Someone must decide who was right, and so the issues went to the courts—the courts of the Church, the courts of the State, and *ad hoc* courts in the Universities.[323]

Pilate's question to Jesus, "What is truth?" (John 18:38) is a question which continues to perplex the church. Many traditionalist Anglicans have maintained that certain new understandings on the part of many in the church, concerning but not limited to the matter of human sexuality, have compromised (to use Hinchcliffe's term) "the faith once delivered to the saints." While the term is widely used, it is an imprecise one. First, it does not specify the saints to whom the faith was delivered. Is this a reference to those officially canonized or are they the *hagioi,* all the people of God, to whom Paul addressed his epistles? When was the "once" when the faith was delivered? Was it Mount Sinai or the Mount of Olives? Was it Nicaea or Chalcedon? Further, who was the deliverer of the truth? And if God, by what means? Theophany? Through the word of prophets? Archbishop Greg Venables of the Southern Cone, for example, has maintained that "a new version of Christianity has evolved—a post-modern, relativistic Christianity," but that this phenomenon has not affected Anglicans in the Global South, who have not wavered from the truth![324]

Leaders of the South African church have consistently maintained that "the truth newly perceived" is not necessarily heretical. Ndungane believes, for example, that "to do theology is to open ourselves to dynamic, vibrant, complex truth," and that this realization leads to an ongoing, un-folding conversation with God, through which we are touched, changed and transformed.[325] Ndungane also sees the newly perceived truth as part of what he calls the church's "journey toward wholeness." Addressing the matter of women's ordination, for example, he maintains that the church has moved to an understanding that it was consonant with the will of God. "The priesthood became more representative of all God's people; women were able to take their rightful place sharing sacramental ministry," a ministry enriched by their presence.[326] In this regard, we are reminded of Bishop Russell's approach to the evolution of biblical theology, in which he makes a distinction between what is true "for the times" and what is true "for all times." We learn from Archbishop Tutu that truth has an even more noble mission. He believes that in the work of the Truth and Reconciliation Commission, the telling of the truth, far more than punitive actions against evildoers, or a misguided attempt to forget the truth, leads to both freedom and stability.[327]

Covenant vs. Contract

Among the difficulties encountered as contemporary Anglicans have tried to deal with the crises that face the church is that the "ground rules" for the conduct of business in Anglican bodies seem to have changed. In the current climate, as I have observed elsewhere, Anglicans seem to be guided less by covenant and more by contract.[328] The Welsh theologian Lorraine Cavanagh observes that Richard Hooker, Anglicanism's chief apologist, understood the church to be "an integrated life of relationships which are continually being transformed by the abiding Spirit of Christ's authority who enables its structure to become a supple and enduring framework holding the Communion together at greater depth."[329] In such a covenantal practice of religion, room was traditionally made under the Anglican umbrella in order that divergent yet complementary views could find shelter there. In such an atmosphere, each province was trusted to run its own affairs. As Hooker himself wrote, "every former part gives strength unto all that follow."[330] And when there were disagreements, those constituent parts followed the counsel of Isaiah, "Come let us reason together, though our sins be like scarlet" (Isaiah 1:18, KJV).

In recent years, however, such a sense of supple covenant has given way to rigid contract. Anglicanism is no longer, as was once envisioned, "an inn where all are received joyously," but is fast becoming "a cottage where some few friends of the family are to be received." In the wake of an escalated level of distrust within the Communion's ranks, a newfound reverence for legalism has emerged, so that in dealing with differences, the default position is no longer deliberation with a possible eye to reconciliation, but a decision to remove from fellowship those who have divergent views.

Many believe that the Archbishop of Canterbury himself has set the tone for such a new approach to Anglicanism and has through his actions empowered other "instruments of unity" within the Communion to do likewise. In light of the new powers acceded to him in the Windsor Report, this comes as no surprise. In a seminal document entitled "Archbishop's Reflections on the Anglican Communion," issued 27 June 2006, Dr. Rowan Williams first expresses a view with which most Anglicans would concur, namely that the Communion "is an association of local churches, not a single organization with a controlling bureaucracy and a universal system of law," with the result that "everything depends on what have generally been unspoken conventions of mutual respect." He goes on to suggest, however, that the decision of the Episcopal Church to consecrate a practicing homosexual falls outside the parameters of such respect. "Actions have consequences," he writes, and further "have the effect of putting a Church outside or even across the central stream of the life they have shared with other churches."

In the section of the document entitled "Future Directions," Dr. Williams states that "the best way forward" for Anglicanism would be a covenant among local churches, which he sees as an attempt to "harmonize" the church law of those bodies.[331] The irony, of course, is that the adoption of such a covenant would result in something akin to a "universal system of law" which, by the archbishop's own admission, is contrary to the ethos of Anglicanism. Moreover, according to the archbishop, the covenant could presage what could be described as a two-tiered Anglicanism made up of "constituent churches in covenant with the Anglican Communion and other churches in association" with it. His statement that such an arrangement would be analogous to the relationship between the Church of England and the Methodist Church, however, strongly suggests that the associate members would not be recognized as Anglicans at all. The archbishop's disclaimer at the end of the document could be read as disingenuous. He states that "the idea of an Archbishop of Canterbury resolving any of this by decree is misplaced" since he "must always act collegially, with the bishops of his own local Church and with the primates and the other instruments of communion." The fact remains, however, that as *primus inter pares*, and as the titular spiritual leader of and spokesperson for some eighty million Anglicans worldwide, the occupant of the Throne of St. Augustine possesses an influence and a moral suasion which can have a profound effect on the deliberations that could affect the future shape of the Anglican Communion.

The language of the proposed Anglican Covenant, drafted by a committee chaired by the Most Reverend Drexel Gomez, Archbishop of the West Indies, builds on the themes of the Archbishop's "Reflections." Indeed, the document may be seen as one whose purpose is to provide both theological and legal justification for relegating some members of the Communion to "associate" status, which, as we have seen, is tantamount to the removal of those members from the Anglican fold. Indeed, the whole document, whose stated purpose is "to hold together and strengthen the life of the Communion" (viz., its constituent membership) seems to find its meaning in its penultimate paragraph:

> We acknowledge that in the most extreme circumstances, where member churches chose not to fulfill the substance as under-stood by the Instruments of Communion, we will consider that such churches will have relinquished for themselves the force and meaning of the covenant's purpose, and a process of restoration and renewal will be required to re-establish their covenant rela-tionship with other member churches.[332]

The proposed Anglican Covenant is problematic for a number of reasons. First, while giving lip service to the autonomy of each province, it asks that each church recognize that it is bound "not juridically by a central or legislative or executive authority, but by the Holy Spirit who calls and enables us to live in mutual loyalty and service." The question immediately raised is who will determine the mind of the Holy Spirit in such matters. The answer is given in the same paragraph of the Covenant, which states, "We affirm the place of four Instruments of Communion [viz., the Archbishop of Canterbury, the Anglican Consultative Council, the Primates and the Lambeth Conference] *which serve to discern our common mind in communion issues,* and to foster our interdependence and mutual accountability in Christ." Having rejected a central and legislative or executive authority, the Covenant seems clearly to ascribe such a function to the Instruments in question. Such a provision threatens, compromises and undermines the time-honored Anglican understanding of provincial autonomy, especially since the draft also provides for the resolution of serious disputes through their arbitration by the Primates, whose role will be to "offer guidance and direction."

The Covenant, if adopted, therefore, will result in what can only be called the curialization of Anglicanism. This represents not only an abandonment of provincial autonomy, but perhaps more important, a rejection of Anglicanism's synodical approach to governance, which honors the contributions of bishops, clergy and laypeople. If we examine the structure of the instruments, we see that laypersons are found only in the membership of the ACC. Indeed, until recently, laypersons made up the majority of that body. This changed, however, at ACC-13, at which a resolution was passed to make all primates *ex officio* members of the Council. This has resulted in a situation in which the influence of clergy and laypeople has been significantly diminished. All four instruments are in the hands of bishops, and in the case of three of them, archbishops.

Primatial Promulgations

Given the tone of the Windsor Report, the expressed opinions of the Archbishop of Canterbury, the decisions of the ACC, and the authority which the proposed Anglican Covenant would cede to the Primates, the actions of the Primates at their February 2007 meeting in Tanzania astonished few observers of recent church history. In their Communiqué, the heads of the provinces of the Anglican Communion endorsed the proposed Anglican Covenant, which would "make explicit what Anglicans mean by 'bonds of affection' and secure the commitment of each Province to those bonds [so that the] structures of our common life can be articulated and enhanced."[333] As a short-term resolution to the problems that have arisen with respect to recent developments in The Episcopal Church, the Primates put forward several recommendations. Principal among these were the establishment of a Pastoral Council of five members which would monitor TEC's response to the Windsor Report, and facilitate and encourage healing and reconciliation within the Episcopal Church, the Episcopal Church and those alienated from it, and the Episcopal Church and the rest of the Anglican Communion; the appointment of a Primatial Vicar who would be responsible to the Council. It is noteworthy that under the proposed scheme, two of the Council's members would be nominated by the Primates, two by the Presiding Bishop, and one, a primate who would serve as chair, by the Archbishop of Canterbury.

Further, the Primates requested that the House of Bishops of the Episcopal Church not authorize any rite for same-sex blessings and that no consent be given for the consecration of a bishop living in a same-sex union. The Primates indicated that failure to comply with these requests would have "consequences for the full participation of the church in the life of the Communion." It is noteworthy that the Communiqué underscored that the American church was bound to comply with these requests *unless* some new consensus emerges in the Anglican Communion.[334]

While the House of Bishops was sympathetic to many of the concerns expressed by the Primates, it rejected the extreme measures put forward to address them. In their statement released following a meeting of the House held in March 2007, the bishops pointed out, *inter alia,* that the delegation of primatial authority was not permissible, and that to adopt the Primates' recommendations would "replace the local governance of the Church by its own people with the decisions of a distant and unaccountable group of prelates."[335] The communication also pointed out a double standard on the part of the Primates, who were quick to excoriate the Episcopal Church for its alleged failure to comply with the Windsor Report, while virtually condoning the actions of Global South Primates who with impunity violated provincial boundaries, and who in so doing also violated the dictates of the Windsor Report.

The Dar es Salaam Communiqué, like most primatial documents issued since the Windsor Report, ostensibly trumpets the cause of unity, but in fact advocates Anglican uniformity. The Primates' Tanzanian pronouncement differs from its predecessors from Windsor, Dromantine and Nassau in degree, not in kind. It is the most unambiguous of all the documents. By drawing a very definitive line in the sand, it narrows the breadth and scope of Anglicanism and by extension makes it clear that in their opinion, fewer and fewer people will have the right to profess and call themselves Anglicans. Quick to cite Lambeth I.10, the 1998 resolution which declared homosexual behavior incompatible with Scripture, the documents have all but ignored the provision in the same resolution for ongoing dialogue with homosexual persons.

South Africa as a Crucible for the Communion

The South African church has been assiduous in its attempts to help the Communion focus on its stated but recently abandoned commitment to unity in diversity. In commenting on the impact of the Windsor Report, Archbishop Ndungane expressed the hope that its recommendations would be taken seriously, "so we can restore a deeper unity to our Communion, and continue, with increased concord and purpose, the mission of Christ's Church."[336] Later, when Dr. Williams offered his "reflections" on Anglicanism in which he suggested that a solution to our current crisis might be an evolution into an Anglicanism with constituent and associate members, Archbishop Ndungane, citing the CPSA's experience in dealing with differences, issued a statement in which he said, "I would like to stress that constant talk of schism from various quarters does not address the heart of the matter which is living with difference and otherness. . . . A proper understanding of how the institutional life of the Anglican Communion has served our spiritual life and ministry is fundamental to avoiding a knee-jerk resorting to talk of schism whenever any disagreements arise among us." In a not-too-veiled reference to the idea of an Anglican covenant, Ndungane declared that "there is a lack of appreciation for the governing structures of the Anglican Communion." In iterating a principle articulated by Archbishop Langley at the first Lambeth Conference, the Archbishop of Cape Town made it clear that "the worldwide Anglican Communion is made up of autonomous provinces which make their own laws."[337]

As Archbishop and Metropolitan of Cape Town, Njongonkulu Ndungane is the successor to the bishop who excommunicated Colenso. But theologically and politically, he is in many ways more closely aligned with the deposed bishop of Natal. First, by Anglican and certainly African standards, Ndungane is undoubtedly in the "liberal" camp, if for different reasons than Colenso. Moreover, he is indebted to Colenso's difficulties. Their resolution provided indirectly the infrastructure of the Communion which gave Ndungane the very rationale for his unprecedented invitation to his brother and sister bishops to hold the Lambeth Conference in Cape Town. Indeed, years hence it may be written of the incumbent archbishop what he himself has said of Colenso: "[He] represents the possibilities for creative dialogue and fusion between the indigenous culture . . . and the emerging global culture of the West."[338]

His role as bridge-builder in Anglicanism has included a commitment to being a spokesperson for what might be called a centrist African position.

He has consistently tried to strike common chords in efforts to unite Anglican Christians. In a sermon marking the inauguration of the companion relationship between his province and the Diocese of Washington, he commented that "partnership is about each having something to give . . . for the rest of the body." He emphasized, too, how all nations, rich and poor, are threatened by infringements on human rights, necessitating a uniting around *Ubuntu* values.[339]

With a sincere effort to bring the Lambeth Conference to South Africa, the Conference has come full circle. After more than a century and a half, South Africa, for demonstrable historical, political and theological reasons, is once again at the eye of the storm. Each in his own age, John William Colenso and Njongonkulu Winston Hugh Ndungane have dared to march to the beat of a different drummer. Colenso could have also written a book entitled "A World with a Human Face." Ndungane encourages people to look beyond the statistics and the homophobia and into the eyes of a gay teenager or those of his parents (as he asked delegates to do at a recent provincial synod). Colenso, in the same way, looked into the eyes of the Zulu and saw not a godless idolater or a subhuman creature, but a child of God with an innate capacity for ethical behavior. On the scriptural front, the two bishops interpreted the Bible in ways unacceptable to the majority of their contemporaries. Bishop Colenso wrote, "The Bible can no longer be regarded as infallibly true in matters of history as well as science."[340] Archbishop Ndungane, who, unlike most of his fellow African primates, upholds the validity of the election of Gene Robinson, wrote:

> It was assumed that the Bible spoke clearly on the issue and that homosexuality is sinful . . . [but] given that the Scriptures were written at least twenty centuries ago, before the advent and development of our current medical, psychological and sociological studies, this attitude towards scripture might validly be accused of being simply a way to support a particular prejudice.[341]

Physicists know that a crucible is a vessel made of a material, such as porcelain, which is refractory, that is, resistant to heat and incapable of melting. It can therefore be used to heat materials to very high temperatures or to melt them. From this scientific definition, two figurative definitions have derived. The first is that of a severe test (for instance of one's patience or faith), a trial, an ordeal. Indeed we often speak of a "fiery ordeal" or a "trial by fire." In our own lifetimes we have seen South Africa as such a crucible. We have seen the suffering, the torture and the inhumane treatment of her citizens, who were systemically denied basic human rights. But we have also witnessed the struggle of those who have withstood the intense heat brought on by degradation, deprivation and destitution. We have witnessed too their emergence from that crucible, tried and strengthened for leadership in a transformed society. Nelson Mandela, a political prisoner for nearly three decades who became the first president of the new South Africa is the icon, embodiment and personification of that struggle. We have also witnessed valiant members of the church during this period, "prisoners of hope," to use Ezekiel's description of God's faithful people, who not only prayed for change, but who labeled apartheid as sin and fought tirelessly for its dismantling.

The second derivative definition of crucible is "a place, time, or situation characterized by the confluence of powerful intellectual, social, economic, political or spiritual forces." South Africa, and particularly, the Church in the Province of Southern Africa, is a crucible in this sense as well. South African church leaders to whom I spoke all described both church and society in South Africa as a microcosm, a people "whose strength," as Bishop Nuttall has described it, "has been in our ability to hold on to one another despite our differences." If their Constitution is any indication, South Africans are a people, if we may borrow a phrase from the Baptismal office, who strive to respect the dignity of every human being.[342]

The issues facing twenty-first century Anglicanism, as we have seen, are not as novel as they would appear. They are old issues in new guises. But the issues in their new incarnation are far more ominous. When Robert Gray left Cape Town to attend Lambeth in 1867, he was away for nearly three months. Two of the months were spent sailing to and from Southampton, the other attending the meetings and looking after other matters in England. Four years separated Colenso's trial and the Lambeth Conference convened to consider the issues raised by it. Today, for most inhabitants of "this fragile earth, our island home," there are few destinations that cannot be reached by the next day. Decisions of synods and commissions and conventions, as well as interpretations of and "spins" on those actions are, thanks to the Internet, communicated instantaneously. In this regard, we were struck by the news that Primates at their meeting in Dromantine were sending and receiving text messages on their cell phones from lobbyists not physically present at the meeting.

"Ex Africa Semper Aliquid Novi"

Pliny the Elder (23–79 A.D.) was a Roman scholar best known for his thirty-seven-volume work, *Naturalis Historia*, an encyclopedia of virtually everything that was known by the ancient world at that time. It contains the oft-quoted phrase, "Ex Africa semper aliquid novi" ("There is always something new coming out of Africa"), by which I think Pliny meant that Africa could always be relied on to spring surprises, by astonishing the world with some significant development.

I think this phrase bears especial relevance to the current crisis in Anglicanism. Surprises from the African continent have been of two kinds. The first is that it has emerged as Anglicanism's new center. On that continent reside most of the world's Anglicans, and as we learned at Lambeth XIII, most of the world's Anglican bishops. No longer residents of colonies established by European powers, Africans are proud citizens of sovereign states. In the place of governors general and viceroys now sit native presidents and prime ministers. In the place of missionary bishops sent to convert the heathen, now sit indigenous bishops. These developments have resulted, understandably, in a sea change in African Anglicanism, and with it a loss, for good or ill, of much of what formerly characterized it. This is because African Anglicanism, indeed global Anglicanism, has moved away from what one theologian calls the "predecessor paradigms" of domestic national imperialism and colonial imperialism.[343]

It would be unreasonable to expect that the sea change would not have theological ramifications. Indeed, one apparent result of the shedding of imperialist "baggage" has been that biblical inerrancy seems to have supplanted the time-honored "three-legged stool" of Scripture, tradition and reason, because the latter two legs were more the product of European thought patterns. Thus, one of the surprises to emerge "ex Africa" is a new problem of a serious theological divergence among Anglicans. This divergence has been, by and large, the impediment to dialogue.

But if such an impediment can be seen as the problem, we must also own that "ex Africa" is emerging the solution, and that solution is the corrective that the South African church has provided. Its unique experiences as a church never far removed from the struggles of the nation in which it found itself have equipped the CPSA to act as bridge builder, sounding board and lightning rod for the Communion. Its particular role in the dismantling of apartheid, and more recently, through the Truth and Reconciliation Commission, as a healer of the post-apartheid nation, means that it is especially well equipped to function in the role of reconciler among sister and brother Anglicans. As Bishop Russell said at a recent Synod, the CPSA has a "pivotal and prophetic role to play in the healing of the present divisions in our communion."

He goes on to say that because the South African church has held together despite having to deal with "highly emotive issues and divisive situations" such as apartheid and women's ordination, they should maintain the same resolve during the present divisions, despite advice to the contrary. He urged the Synod delegates: "Let us be faithful to such prophetic witness."[344]

Clearly, the Church in the Province of Southern Africa is equal to the task of being the crucible of twenty-first century Anglicanism.

Notes

1   A province is a group of at least five (normally geographically contiguous) dioceses. It may be an entire country, such as the Episcopal Church in the United States, the Anglican Church of Canada, or the Eglise Episcopale du Congo. Or it may be made up of a group of neighboring countries, such as the Province of West Africa or the Province of the West Indies. At present there are thirty-nine such provinces in the Anglican Communion, representing a total membership of more than eighty million Anglicans dispersed among more than one hundred countries.

2   The Most Rev. Howard H. Clark, Archbishop of Rupert's Land, cited in James B. Simpson and Edward M. Story, *The Long Shadows of Lambeth X* (New York: McGraw Hill, 1969), 280.

3   Draft resolution on violence, Lambeth Conference, 1968, cited in Simpson and Story, *The Long Shadows*, 127.

4   Lambeth Conference, 1988, Resolution 39.

5   Archbishop Njongonkulu Ndungane, "Remarks to the Lambeth Plenary on International Debt," Anglican Communion News Service (25 July 1998).

6   The Province of Southern Africa, in addition to South Africa, includes Namibia, Angola, Lesotho, Mozambique, Swaziland and the Island of St. Helena.

7   "2008 Lambeth Conference goes to Canterbury," *Christianity Today* (17 December 2004).

8   "Britain can't be called Christian, says Archbishop [of York David Hope]" *The Sunday Times* (12 December 2004).

9   The SPG was founded in 1701 to provide overseas chaplaincies for English families abroad, and to evangelize African slaves in North America and the Caribbean. The original chaplains to the American colonies were SPG missionaries. The SPG's enterprise later spread to West and Southern Africa. In ministering to slaves, it should be noted, the SPG insisted that slaves were "human beings equal to whites in every endowment

and capable of salvation, education and general uplift." Nevertheless, it "accepted slavery as a vital factor in British prosperity." See J. Carleton Hayden, "Afro-Anglican Linkages, 1701–1900: Ethiopia Shall Soon Stretch Out Her Hands unto God," *Journal of Religious Thought*, Vol. 44, No. 1 (1987): 25.

10 Anglican Communion News Service 3918, 10 December 2004.

11 Burundi, Central Africa, Congo, Indian Ocean, Kenya, Nigeria, Rwanda, South Africa, Sudan, Tanzania, Uganda, and West Africa. The Diocese of Egypt is part of the Episcopal Church of Jerusalem and the Middle East.

12 David Hamid, "The Nature and Shape of the Contemporary Anglican Communion, in Ian Douglas and Kwok Pui-Lan, *Beyond Colonial Anglicanism*, 81–82.

13 R. William Franklin, "Lambeth 1998 and the Future Mission of the Episcopal Church," *Anglican Theological Review*, Vol. 81, Number 2 (Spring 1999), 262.

14 Njongonkulu Ndungane, *A World with a Human Face: A Voice from Africa* (Cape Town: David Philip Publishers, 2003), 110–111.

15 The Church Missionary Society was founded in 1799. One of its founders was William Wilberforce, known for his indefatigable and successful struggle in Parliament for the abolition of slavery. It pioneered missionary work in Canada, New Zealand, and Africa, esp. E. Africa. "From its earliest days the Society's theology has been consistently Evangelical." (*Oxford Dictionary of the Christian Church*, 1978.)

16 George Washington Doane, "Fling out the banner," and Reginald Heber, "From Greenland's icy mountains," *The Hymnal 1940,* 259 and 254 respectively.

17 See Josiah H. Idowu-Fearon, "The Challenge of Islam in Northern Nigeria," *Anglican Theological Review*, Vol. LXXVII, No. 4 (Fall 1995), 543–544.

18 Kwok Pui-Lan, "The Legacy of Cultural Hegemony," eds. Ian Douglas and Kwok Pui-Lan, *Beyond Colonial Anglicanism* (New York: Church Publishing, 2001), 49.

19 Kortright Davis, "As we sail life's rugged sea," Ian Douglas and Kwok Pui-Lan, eds., *Beyond Colonial Anglicanism*, 125ff.

20 Luke Pato, "Becoming an African Church," Frank England and Torquil Paterson, eds., *Bounty in Bondage: the Anglican Church in Southern Africa*

(Johannesburg: Raven Press 1989), 159. See also Pato, "Indigenisation and Liberation: A Challenge to Theology in the South African Context," *Journal of Theology for Southern Africa* 99 (1997) 40–46.

21 Njongonkulu Ndungane, "Scripture: What is at issue in Anglicanism Today?" Ian Douglas and Kwok Pui-Lan, eds., *Beyond Colonial Anglicanism*, 239.

22 See, e.g., James Cone, *God of the Oppressed,* (New York: Seabury, 1975); Gustavo Gutierrez, *A Theology of Liberation: History, Politics and Salvation,* (Maryknoll, NY: Orbis, 1988); John Pobee, *Who Are the Poor? The Beatitudes as a Call to Community,* (Geneva: World Council of Churches, 1988); Chukwudum Okolo, *African Liberation Theology: Challenges for the Church in Africa,* (Lagos: Fulladu Publishing, 1997).

23 The first conference, "Afro-Anglicanism: Present Issues, Future Tasks," was held at Codrington College, Barbados in 1985; the second, "Afro-Anglicanism: Identity, Integrity and Impact in the Decade of Evangelism," was held at the University of the Western Cape, Cape Town, South Africa in 1995, and the most recent, "Celebrating the Gifts of Afro-Anglicanism," was held in 2005 at the University of Toronto.

24 Harold T. Lewis, "They call them to deliver their land from error's chain," Opening address, Second International Conference on Afro-Anglicanism, *Anglican Theological Review,* Vol. LXXVII, No. 4 (Fall, 1995), 458.

25 Harry Emerson Fosdick, "God of grace and God of glory," *The Hymnal 1982,* 594.

26 Reginald Heber, "From Greenland's icy mountains," *The Hymnal 1940*, 254

27 Njongonkulu Ndungane, *A World with a Human Face*, 110.

28 The question is a real one. Some African primates have vowed to absent themselves if American bishops are invited. In April 2007, the Primate of Canada suggested that the Archbishop of Canterbury not convene Lambeth, pending a "cooling off period."

29 Jonathan A. Draper, "Bishop John William Colenso and History as Unfolding Narrative," *Journal of Theology for Southern Africa*, 117, (November 2003), 100.

30 "Lambeth Conference goes to Canterbury," *Christianity Today* (17 December 2004).

31 It is noteworthy that the request, drafted by Bishop Lewis of Ontario, suggested that the bishops be "attended by one or more of their Presbyters or Laymen, learned in Ecclesiastical law, as their advisers." But in the end, only bishops were invited.

32 Jonathan A. Draper, "Colenso's *Commentary on Romans*: An Exegetical Assessment," in Draper, ed. *The Eye of the Storm: Bishop John William Colenso and the Crisis of Biblical Interpretation* (Pietermaritzburg: Cluster Publications, 2003), 105.

33 Cecil Lewis and G. E. Edwards. *Historical Records of the Church in the Province of South Africa* (London: SPCK, 1934), 320.

34 The Privy Council was constituted in 1833 as a Court of Appeals, and since the Church of England was the established church, had jurisdiction over its disputes. It gained much notoriety through a series of ritual and doctrinal cases brought before it in the nineteenth century. (See *Oxford Dictionary of the Christian Church*.)

35 Lewis and Edwards, *Historical Records*, 171–2.

36 The Privy Council, in effect, supported Colenso's contention that Gray had arrogated authority to himself which had not been conferred on him and which was not inherent in his office. The issue revolves around the question of whether Gray was a metropolitan, i.e., a bishop exercising provincial and not merely diocesan powers. The language of the Lambeth documents accords Gray that title, and refers to Colenso as his suffragan, but the Privy Council apparently regarded the two bishops as bishops of their respective sees, each with jurisdiction and the rights and privileges inherent in the office.

37 cited in Peter Hinchcliff, *John William Colenso, Bishop of Natal* (London: Nelson, 1964), 166.

38 Maritzburg was a shortened form and common nickname for Pietermaritzburg, the see city of the Diocese of Natal. Strictly speaking, Maritzburg did not exist at all!

39 Twenty-three bishops came from England and Ireland; six from Scotland; twenty-four from the English colonies (Bishop Colenso was not invited); nineteen from the American Episcopal Church. Four retired colonial bishops resident in England were also present. The only black bishop at the time, Samuel Adjai Crowther, who had been consecrated in 1864 for the Church in Nigeria, was not in attendance.

40   cited in Alan M.G. Stephenson, *Anglicanism and the Lambeth Conferences* (London: SPCK, 1978), 39.

41   Until 1926, the presiding bishopric of ECUSA was held the senior bishop in the House in terms of years of service, a distinction held in 1867 by Bishop Hopkins of Vermont. Beginning in 1926, presiding bishops were elected, but it wasn't until 1944, with the election of Henry St. George Tucker, Bishop of Virginia, that a presiding bishop was required to resign as bishop of his diocese. In light of recent developments in the Anglican Communion, we can appreciate the irony of Bishop Hopkins' motion to excommunicate Colenso.

42   cited in Stephenson, *Lambeth Conference,* 263–264.

43   Hinchcliff, *Colenso*, 185. A committee of seven bishops was named, with the right to co-opt "men learned in Ecclesiastical and Canon Law." The committee included Selwyn, Gray and Hopkins.

44   Hinchcliff, *Colenso,* 143.

45   Letter from Pusey to Bishop Archibald Tait of London (later Archbishop of Canterbury) cited in Gwilym Colenso, "The Pentateuch in Perspective: Bishop Colenso's Biblical Criticism in its Colonial Context," in ed. Jonathan Draper, *The Eye of the Storm*, 137.

46   Philippe Dennis, "Introduction," Draper, ed., *Eye of the Storm,* 2.

47   Michael Nuttall, *Number Two to Tutu: A Memoir* (Pietermaritzburg: Cluster Publications), 2003, 112.

48   This and subsequent comments were expressed by Jonathan Draper in an interview with the author at University of KwaZulu Natal, Pietermaritzburg, 28 July 2005.

49   This and subsequent comments were expressed by Bishop Michael Nuttall in an interview with the author in Pietermaritzburg, 29 July 2005.

50   Interview with Archbishop Njongonkulu Ndungane, Toronto, 21 July 2005.

51   Jeff Guy, *The Heretic: A Study of the Life of John William Colenso, 1814–1883* (Pietermaritzburg: Raven Press, 1983), 77.

52   Ronald B. Nicholson, "Other Times and Other Customs: A Storm in a Victorian Teacup?" in ed. Draper, *Eye of the Storm,* 179.

53   See esp. Jonathan Draper, "The Trial of Bishop John William Colenso," in ed. Draper, *Eye of the Storm,* 306ff.

54   Resolution 72: Exculpation of John William Colenso, Second Agenda

Book, page 22. Minutes of the 30th Session of the Provincial Synod of the CPSA, Bloemfontein, South Africa, 26 September 2002. It should be noted that Archbishop Ndungane declared this a controversial matter, and ordered that a vote be taken by houses, meaning that a two-thirds vote by each house, bishops, priests and laypersons (and not a simple majority of all present) would be necessary for the resolution to pass. Such a parliamentary procedure helps to ensure that potentially weighty matters have overwhelming support.

55 Jonathan Draper, "Bishop John William Colenso and History as Unfolding Narrative," *Journal of Theology for Southern Africa*, 117, (November 2003), 104.

56 Michael Nuttall, "The Province of Southern Africa," Charles Hefling and Cynthia Shattuck, eds., *The Oxford Guide to the Book of Common Prayer: A Worldwide Survey* (New York: Oxford University Press, 2006), 319.

57 Peter Hinchcliff, *The Anglican Church in South Africa: An account of the history and development of the Church in the Province of South Africa* (London: Darton, 1963), 71.

58 John W. deGrucy, *The Church Struggle in South Africa* (Grand Rapids, Eerdmans), 1979, 17.

59 Jonathan Draper, "Bishop John William Colenso and History as Unfolding Narrative," *Journal of Theology for Southern Africa,* 117 (November 2003), 100.

60 Gray, in fact, had established Zonnebloem College in Cape Town, a school for the sons of African chiefs that was expressly designed to take them out of their traditional culture and turn them into good Anglicans fit for English society.

61 Jonathan Draper, Introduction, *Commentary on Romans by Bishop John William Colenso.* (Pietermaritzburg: Cluster Publications, 2003), xi.

62 Guy, *The Heretic,* 43.

63 Ibid, 134.

64 Luke Pato, "Becoming an African Church," in England and Paterson, *Bounty in Bondage,* 169–70.

65 Eleanor Johnson and John Clark, eds., *Anglicans in Mission: A Transforming Journey,* Report of the Mission Commission of the Anglican Communion, to the Anglican Consultative Council, Edinburgh, September, 1999 (London: SPCK, 2000), 27–28.

66 Jonathan Draper. "Bishop John William Colenso and History as Unfolding Narrative," *Journal of Theology for Southern Africa,* 117 (November 2003), 103.

67 Livingstone Ngewu, "Colenso and the Enigma of Polygamy," in ed. Draper, *Eye of the Storm,* 296.

68 Hinchcliff, *The Anglican Church in South Africa,* 121.

69 Archbishop Desmond Tutu, in the Foreword to Frank England and Torquil Paterson, eds., *Bounty in Bondage: The Anglican Church in Southern Africa* (Johannesburg: Raven Press, 1989), v.

70 Geoffrey Faber, *Oxford Apostles: A Character Study of the Oxford Movement* (London: Faber & Faber, 1936), 84–85.

71 P.E. More and F. L. Cross, *Anglicanism* (London: SPCK, 1935), xxx.

72 Ibid., lxii.

73 When Elizabeth I, daughter of Henry VIII and Anne Boleyn, acceded to the throne in 1558, one of the main difficulties was the question of her religion. The country was predominantly Catholic, though with strong Calvinist undercurrents. Elizabeth disliked the former because it denied her legitimacy, and the latter because it had abolished the episcopacy, which she held to be essential for the protection of monarchs. She therefore aimed at a compromise between the Lutheran political theory (with its emphasis on the prerogatives of temporal rulers) and the episcopal organization of Catholicism, many of whose institutions and practices she intended to retain. Many of these adjustments were more formally recognized in the 1559 Prayer Book.

74 Frank England, "Tracing Southern African Anglicanism," in *Bounty and Bondage*, ed. England and Paterson, 16.

75 1928 Book of Common Prayer of the Episcopal Church USA, Service of the Ordination of a Priest, 546.

76 The phrase itself, a twentieth-century invention, does not actually appear in Hooker's writings. But the theology behind the phrase is present in his writings: "What Scripture doth plainly deliver, to that first place both of credit and obedience is due; the next whereunto is whatsoever any man can necessarily conclude by force of reason; after these the voice of the Church succeedeth. That which the Church by her ecclesiastical authority shall probably think and define to be true or good, must in congruity of reason over-rule all other inferior judgments whatsoever"

(Laws, Book V, 8:2; Folger Edition 2:39, 8–14).

77   Faber, *Oxford Apostles*, 342.

78   See J. H. Newman, *Apologia pro Vita Sua* (London: A. and C. Black, 1864), 65.

79   J.H.R. Moorman, *A History of the Church in England.* (London: A. and C. Black, 1953), 335.

80   Yngve Brilioth, *The Anglican Revival: Studies in the Oxford Movement* (London: Longmans, Green, 1933), 20.

81   England, "Tracing Southern African Anglicanism," 22.

82   Richard Holloway, *The Anglican Tradition* (Wilton, Conn.: Morehouse-Barlow, 1984), 40ff.

83   Peter Hinchcliff, *The Anglican Church in South Africa: An account of the history and development of the Church in the Province of South Africa* (London: Darton, 1963), 231.

84   cited in J.R. Wright, *Lift High the Cross* (Cincinnati: Forward Movement Publications, 1984), 101.

85   Holloway, *The Anglican Tradition,* 41.

86   See Hinchcliff, *The Anglican Church in South Africa*, 191.

87   H. R. T. Brandreth, OGS, "A History of the Oratory of the Good Shepherd," http://anglicanhistory.org/misc/ogs.html.

88   Although conditions have improved considerably, the current health concern is that the hostel system exacerbates the AIDS pandemic, as men far from home are more likely to avail themselves of prostitutes or, as is often the case in enforced same-sex environments, engage in sex with each other.

89   Alan Paton, *Apartheid and the Archbishop: The Life and Times of Geoffrey Clayton* (New York: Charles Scribner's Sons, 1973), 156.

90   Fr. Alban Winter, CR, cited in John Allen, *Rabble-Rouser for Peace, the Authorized Biography of Desmond Tutu* (London: Random House, 2006), 32.

91   St. Peter's moved from Rosettenville to Johannesburg to Alice, in the Eastern Cape. There were three other institutions where (mostly white) ordinands were trained: the Federal Theological Seminary (FEDSEM) at Imbali near Pietermaritzburg, St. Bede's, Umtata, and St. Paul's, Grahamstown. In the early 1990s, owing to declining enrollment and rising operational costs, the bishops of the province consolidated the seminaries, and inaugurated the College of the Transfiguration, now the

official seminary of the CPSA, which occupies the former St. Paul's campus. It should be noted, however, that a goodly number of ordinands from South African dioceses, particularly those for whom ordained ministry is a second vocation, are trained through the (non-residential) Theological Education by Extension (TEE) scheme.

92   Allen, *Rabble-Rouser for Peace*, 170.

93   The Fathers' commitment to indigenous clergy was not limited to their efforts in South Africa. Early in the twentieth century, the Mirfield Fathers founded a seminary for working class men in England who could not afford to attend the church's theological colleges in Oxford, Cambridge and elsewhere. The Fathers also taught for many years at Codrington College, Barbados, the oldest Anglican seminary in the Western hemisphere.

94   Njongonkulu Ndungane, *A World with a Human Face: A Voice from Africa* (Cape Town: David Philip Publishers, 2003), 83.

95   Interview with Archbishop Tutu, Cape Town, August 4, 2004.

96   Michael Battle, *The Ubuntu Theology of Desmond Tutu* (Cleveland: Pilgrim Press, 1997), 91.

97   England, "Tracing Southern African Anglicanism," 19.

98   Ibid.

99   Torquil Paterson, "A Liturgy for Liberation," in ed. England and Paterson, *Bounty in Bondage*, 54.

100   Michael Battle, *Reconciliation: The Ubuntu Theology of Desmond Tutu* (Cleveland: Pilgrim Press, 1997), 87.

101   Mandy Goedhals, "From Paternalism to Partnership: The Church of the Province of Southern Africa and Mission 1848–1988," in *Bounty in Bondage: the Anglican Church in Southern Africa,* ed. Frank England and Torquil Paterson, (Johannesburg: Raven Press, 1989), 105.

102   Desmond Tutu, sermon preached 9 October 1988, cited in John Allen, *Rabble-Rouser for Peace: The Authorised Biography of Desmond Tutu* (London: Random House, 2006), 31.

103   Reginald Heber, "From Greenland's icy mountains," *The Hymnal 1940*, 254.

104   Anthony Grant, *The Past and prospective extension of the gospel by missions to the heathen* (London: Rivington, 1844).

105   Goedhals, "From Paternalism to Partnership," 105.

106 Michael Nuttall, *Number Two To Tutu: A Memoir* (Pietermaritzburg: Cluster Publications, 2003), 111.

107 Goedhals, "From Paternalism to Partnership," 112.

108 Minutes of the Provincial Ministry Conference, 1923, cited in Goedhals "From Paternalism to Partnership," 114 in England and Paterson *Bounty in Bondage.*

109 cited in Peter Hinchcliff, *Anglican Church in South Africa: An Account of the history and development of the Church in the Province of Southern Africa* (London: Darton, 1963), 196.

110 Frank England, "Tracing Southern African Anglicanism," in Frank England and Torquil Paterson, eds., *Bounty in Bondage: the Anglican Church in Southern Africa* (Johannesburg: Raven Press 1989),117.

111 David Hinderer, an English missionary in West Africa commented at the time, "Not that I should have the slightest objection to Bishop Crowther being over myself and the congregation which God may give me . . . But because God gives us influence as Europeans among them, if they hear that a black man is our master, they will question our respectability." See Harold T. Lewis, *Yet With a Steady Beat: The African American Struggle for Recognition in the Episcopal Church* (Valley Forge, Pa.: Trinity Press International, 1996), 81–83.

112 Edward Thomas Demby of Arkansas and Henry Beard Delany of North Carolina were consecrated in 1918, with the understanding that they would only minister to "colored" congregations in the Episcopal Church. See Lewis, *Yet With a Steady Beat,* esp. ch. 5, "The Question of a Racial Episcopate in a Catholic Church."

113 England, "Tracing Southern African Anglicanism," 121.

114 Again, this was a universal Anglican phenomenon. In 1934, in the Episcopal Church USA the Committee on the Status of the Negro declared: "The status of the Negro as regards the spiritual privileges in the Church are the same as those of white clergy and congregations." See Lewis, *Yet With a Steady Beat,* 137.

115 Until the consecration of Bill Burnett, a South African-born white, to the see of Bloemfontein in 1957, all of the bishops in South Africa had been born in England.

116 Cecil Frances Alexander, "All things bright and beautiful," hymn text 1848. This stanza, owing to changing social concepts, was omitted from

the 1940 Hymnal (See *The Hymnal Companion*, 202.)

117   Similarly, it was not until the historic U.S. Supreme Court decision *Brown vs. Board of Education* in 1954, which made segregated educational facilities illegal, that the Episcopal Church moved to integrate its church schools.

118   Goedhals, "From Paternalism to Partnership," 119.

119   Ibid.

120   In 1953, the bishops wrote: "In present circumstances it is reasonable that there should be separate schools for different races. . . But we greatly desire a change in public opinion which would make it possible for some children of all race groups to be educated together." (*Eastern Province Herald*, 27 October 1953).

121   James Cochrane, "Christian Resistance to Apartheid," in ed. Martin Prozesky, *Christianity Amidst Apartheid: Selective Perspectives on the Church in South Africa* (New York: St. Martin's Press, 1990), 86.

122   John W. DeCruchy, *The Church Struggle in South Africa* (Grand Rapids: Erdmans, 1986), 59. This is a phenomenon which has parallels in the attitudes of the Episcopal Church USA at the time of the American civil rights movement. "The Church, then, which historically had turned a deaf ear to the complaints of blacks and had moved slowly and reticently when it did act, now found itself making major concessions [because] the actual motivation to change originated outside the church, where the societal order was undergoing a virtual metamorphosis." (Lewis, *Yet With a Steady Beat,* 161.)

123   Bob Clarke, "Confronting the Crisis: Church-State Relations," in *Bounty in Bondage,* ed. England, 130.

124   Charles Gore, *The Social Gospel of the Sermon on the Mount* (London: Percival, 1893), 9.

125   Luke Pato, "Becoming an African Church," in *Bounty in Bondage,* ed. England, 164.

126   England, "Tracing Southern African Anglicanism," 15.

127   Ibid.

128   Goedhals, "From Paternalism to Partnership," 111.

129   England, "Tracing Southern African Anglicanism," 15.

130   Alan Paton, *Apartheid and the Archbishop* (Cape Town: David Philip, 1973), 9.

131 Goedhals, "From Paternalism to Partnership," 121.

132 For a full discussion of the apartheid system, see, e.g., Leonard Thompson, *A History of South Africa* (New Haven: Yale University Press, 1990), ch. 6.

133 See James L. Gibson, *Overcoming Apartheid: Can Truth Reconcile A Divided Nation?* (New York: Russell Sage Foundation, 2004).

134 Gwendolen M. Carter, *The Politics of Inequality: South Africa Since 1948* (New York: Praeger, 1962), 269, emphasis mine.

135 Ibid., 101.

136 Njongonkulu Ndungane, *A World With a Human Face* (Cape Town: David Philip, 2003), 9. In an address to Parliament in 1953, Dr. Verwoerd, the Minister of Native Affairs, stated: "Racial relations cannot improve if the wrong type of education is given to Natives. . . . It simply creates people who are trained for professions not open to them. . . .What is the use of teaching the Bantu child mathematics when it cannot use it in practice? What is the use of subjecting a Native child to a curriculum which in the first instance is traditionally European? . . . If the Native inside South Africa today in any kind of school in existence is being taught to expect that he will live his adult life under a policy of equal rights he is making a big mistake."

137 Goedhals, "From Paternalism to Partnership," 119.

138 cited in Michael E. Worsnip, *Between Two Fires: The Anglican Church and Apartheid, 1948-1957* (Pietermaritzburg: University of Natal Press, 1991), 93.

139 Paton, *Apartheid and the Archbishop*, 50–52 et passim.

140 T.R.H. Davenport, *South Africa: A Modern History* (Johannesburg: Blackwell Publishing, 1977) 254.

141 B. Bunting, *The Rise of the South African Reich* (London: Penguin African Library, 1964), 118–119.

142 John W. DeGruchy, *The Church Struggle in South Africa* (Grand Rapids: Eerdmans, 1979), 54.

143 Kenneth Hylson-Smith, *High Churchmanship in the Church of England* (Edinburgh: T&T Clark, 1993), 306.

144 For an outline of Scott's ministry, see Bob Clarke, "Confronting the Crisis: Church-State Relations," in *Bounty in Bondage*, ed. England, 131ff.

145 For God's sake wake up!" *The Observer*, 30 August 1953, cited in Worsnip, *Between Two Fires*, 96.

146 Desmond Tutu, "Naught for Your Comfort" inaugural lecture, Church of Christ the King, Sophiatown, 7 August 2004, np.

147 *Eastern Province Herald*, 27 October 1953.

148 Comments made in an address at the "Naught for Your Comfort" inaugural lecture, Church of Christ the King, Sophiatown, 7 August 2004.

149 Robert Denniston, *Trevor Huddleston: A Life* (New York: St. Martin's Press, 2004), 32.

150 Desmond Tutu, "Naught for Your Comfort" inaugural lecture, Church of Christ the King, Sophiatown, 7 August 2004.

151 Aelred Stubbs, CR, "Trevor Huddleston, CR (1913–1998)" Mirfield, Yorks: CR Newsletter, 2000.

152 Ibid.

153 Dennison, *Trevor Huddleston, A Life*, 54.

154 Ibid.

155 Desmond Tutu, "An Appreciation of the Rt. Revd Trevor Huddleston, CR." in Deborah Duncan Honore, *Trevor Huddleston: Essays on his Life and Work* (Oxford University Press, 1988), 3.

156 Goedhals, "From Paternalism to Partnership," 121.

157 cited in Worsnip, *Between Two Fires*, 136–137.

158 Payton, *Apartheid and the Archbishop*, 293.

159 Ibid., 297.

160 Trevor Huddleston was bishop of Stepney from 1968 to 1978, having been translated from Masai, Tanzania.

161 John Stuart Peart-Binns, *Archbishop Joost de Blank: Scourge of Apartheid* (London: Blond and White, 1987), 47.

162 Ibid., 69.

163 George Mukuka, School of Theology, University of Natal, "The Impact of Black Consciousness on Black Catholic Clergy and their Seminary Training," 1972.

164 Ambrose Reeves, "State and Church in South Africa" from Notes and Documents, March 1972.

165 Ibid.

166 De Gruchy, *The Church Struggle in South Africa*, 101.

167   Ibid., 142. (De Gruchy was the first incumbent of the Robert Selby Taylor chair of Christian Studies at the University of Cape Town.)

168   *Adelaide [Australia] Review,* 19 November 2005.

169   Cyprian of Carthage, *De Unitate Catholicae Ecclesiae.*

170   Desmond Tutu, "God-given dignity and the quest for liberation in the light of the South African dilemma," *Liberation,* papers of the 8th National Conference of the SACC, July, 1959, 59, emphasis mine.

171   *Sermo CCCXL.*

172   Michael Battle. *Reconciliation: The Ubuntu Theology of Desmond Tutu* (Cleveland: Pilgrim Press, 1997), 174.

173   Desmond Tutu, "The Theologian and the Gospel of Freedom," *The Trial of Faith: Theology and the Church Today,* ed. Peter Eaton. (Wilton, CT: Churchman Publishing, 1988), 61.

174   Michael Battle, *The Wisdom of Desmond Tutu* (Louisville: Westminster John Knox Press), 1998, 6.

175   Shirley DuBoulay, *Tutu: Voice of the Voiceless* (Grand Rapids: Eerdmans, 1988, 18.

176   Ph.D. dissertation, Union Theological Seminary, 1992.

177   Desmond Tutu, Keynote address delivered at the inaugural "Naught for Your Comfort" Lecture, in honor of Bishop Trevor Huddleston, CR, Christ the King Parish, Sophiatown, 7 August 2004.

178   Ibid.

179   Ibid.

180   Peter Lee, *Compromise and Courage: Anglicans in Johannesburg 1864–1999* (Pietermaritzburg: Cluster Publications, 2005), 389. Bishop Lee was one of the contenders for the bishopric of Johannesburg when Tutu was elected. He is now bishop of the Diocese of Christ the King.

181   cited in DuBoulay, *Tutu, Voice of the Voiceless,* 211.

182   Lee, *Compromise and Courage,* 375.

183   Michael Nuttall, *Number Two to Tutu: A Memoir,* (Pietermaritz: Cluster Publications, 2003), 16.

184   cited in Battle, *Reconciliation,* 8.

185   Desmond Tutu, in James S. Murray's interview, "Racism: We need a prophet," *The Australian,* 10 May 1984.

186   Battle, *Reconciliation,* 8.

187   DuBoulay, *Tutu: Voice of the Voiceless,* 114.

188 Battle, *Reconciliation*, 5.

189 For a full discussion of the topic, see Michael Battle, *Reconciliation: The Ubuntu Theology of Desmond Tutu.*

190 Desmond Tutu, "S.A. Government Hits Council of Churches Administration," *Church & Nation* (Australia) 2 May 1984, 4.

191 John Allen, *Rabble-Rouser for Peace: The Authorised Biography of Desmond Tutu* (London: Random House: 2006), 169–70.

192 The Rev. Roy Snyman, rector of St. Boniface Church, Germiston, cited in Allen, 166.

193 Interview with Bishop Nuttall, Pietermaritzburg, 29 July 2005.

194 Nuttall, *Number Two to Tutu,* 30.

195 Bishopscourt Update Item No. 467, 28 August 1992, CPSA Press Office.

196 Ibid.

197 Njongonkulu Ndungane, *A World with a Human Face* (Cape Town: David Philip, 2003), 16.

198 Nuttall, *Number Two to Tutu,* ch. 14.

199 The murder in question had to be politically motivated and/or committed in response to an order by the apartheid state or some political organization. Those who killed because of personal greed were not entitled to amnesty.

200 Kevin Avruch and Beatriz Vejarano, "Truth and Reconciliation Commissions: A Review Essay and Annotated Bibliography," *Online Journal of Peace and Conflict Resolution,* 4.2, (Spring 2002), 40.

201 Reed Brody, "Justice: The First Casualty of Truth," in *The Nation*, April 30, 2001.

202 Biko, a staunch advocate of black consciousness, was killed while in police custody in September 1977. Tutu was the preacher at Biko's funeral service in King William's Town in the Eastern Cape, which attracted some fifteen thousand mourners, including diplomats from twelve Western countries.

203 Ndungane, *A World With a Human Face*, 19.

204 Desmond Tutu, *No Future Without Forgiveness* (New York: Doubleday, 1999), 31.

205 Ibid., chapter 2.

206 Desmond Tutu, "Where is now thy God?" Address at Trinity Institute Conference, New York, 8 January 1989.

207 Alex Boraine, *A Country Unmasked: Inside South Africa's Truth and Reconciliation*.(Oxford University Press, 2000), 17, emphasis mine.

208 Response by Archbishop Tutu on his appointment as Chairperson of the Truth and Reconciliation Commission, Pretoria, November 30, 1995.

209 Tutu, *No Future Without Forgiveness,* 265.

210 Ibid., 270ff.

211 Ibid., 39.

212 Reed Brody, "Justice:The First Casualty of Truth?: The global movement to end impunity for human rights abuses faces a daunting question." *The Nation,* April 30, 2001.

213 See Avruch and Vejarano, "Truth and Reconciliation Commissions," 37.

214 Interview with Bishop Thabo, Grahamstown, 2 August 2004.

215 Archbishop's charge delivered at Pinetown, KwaZulu Natal, 3 July 2005.

216 "[Drug] corporations continue to use patent protections to ensure high prices, even though five million South Africans are HIV positive and will die early because the drugs are unaffordable." (*World with a Human Face*, 24.)

217 According to Canon Luke Pato, the CPSA and Archbishop Ndungane are highly respected by the SACC and the South African ecumenical community. The SACC often looks to the CPSA to speak on behalf of all Christian churches in South Africa. (Interview, Johannesburg, 8 August 2005.)

218 Thabo Makgoba, bishop of Grahamstown, in an interview, 2 August 2004, Grahamstown.

219 Njongonkulu Ndungane, charge delivered at the Synod of the Church in the Province of Southern Africa, Kwazulu Natal, September 2005.

220 Njongonkulu Ndungane, Sermon preached at the 3rd International Conference on Afro-Anglicanism, St. James' Cathedral, Toronto, July 2005, *Anglican Theological Review,* Vol. 89, No. 1 (2007), 21ff.

221 Njongonkulu Ndungane, Sermon preached in St. George's Cathedral, Cape Town, 14 April 2005 at an interfaith service marking the Global Week of Action on Trade.

222 *The World Fact Book.*

223 Servaas van der Berg, et al., "Trends in poverty and inequality since the political transition," Bureau for Economic Research (BER), University of Stellenbosch: 5 January 2006.

224 Njongonkulu Ndungane, *A World with a Human Face* (Cape Town: David Philip, 2003), 34.

225 Ndungane, *World with a Human Face,* 53.

226 Harold T. Lewis, *Christian Social Witness.* (Cambridge: Cowley Publications, 2001), 74.

227 Njongonkulu Ndungane, 'Towards a Better Life for All the People of Africa," Keynote address, Trade, Aid, and Debt: Toward Economic Justice in Africa – A Consultation for Faith Communities, Washington, June 4–6, 1999.

228 Address by Archbishop Ndungane at the Primates Meeting, Kanuga Conference Center, Hendersonville, North Carolina, USA, 7 March 2001.

229 ACNS Press Release, LC050 (26 July 1998.)

230 Matthew Davis, "Overcoming poverty is focus of interfaith vigil." Episcopal News Service (ENS 091605-2, 16 September 2005. The other MDGs are: achieve universal primary education; promote gender equality and empower women; reduce child mortality; improve maternal health; combat HIV/AIDS, malaria and other diseases; ensure environmental sustainability; and develop a global partnership for development.

231 Archbishop Ndungane, "Statement on Poverty for Religious Leaders' Consultation on Poverty," 11–13 September 2005.

232 Address to Primates, 7 March 2001.

233 ACNS 3960, 18 March 2005.

234 Canon Pato, interview in Johannesburg, 8 August 2005.

235 Lucy Chumbley, "Fighting AIDS: South African visitors share concerns about disease's spread." *Washington Window* (Diocese of Washington) Vol. 73, No. 4 (March 2004), 1.

236 Ibid.

237 "The Church is failing on AIDS, warns Ndungane," Reuters NewMedia, 8 June 2004.

238 Ibid.

239 Chumbley, "Fighting AIDS: South African visitors share concerns," 1.

240 Address at the Opening Service of the 125th anniversary celebration of the Mother's Union, Grahamstown Cathedral, Women's Day, 9 August 2001.

241 "Anglican leader slams South Africa over AIDS drug strategy," Agence

France-Presse, 25 January 2002.

242 "South African Anglican Bishop tells WTO 'start playing fair,'" Ecumenical News International, 20 April 2005.

243 "The Challenge of HIV/AIDS to Christian Theology," University of the Western Cape, 30 July 2004.

244 Ndungane, *A World With a Human Face,* 100–101.

245 Address to the 125th anniversary celebration of the Mother's Union, Grahamstown Cathedral, 9 August 2001.

246 Philip Turner, "Faithful Church, Plural World," *Anglican Theological Review*, Vol. 81, No. 2 (1999), 241.

247 Mazoe Nopece, *Lindaba* (newsletter of the Diocese of Port Elizabeth), January 2005.

248 Ndungane, *A World With a Human Face,* 98.

249 Most biographical information in this section is gleaned from *A World With a Human Face*.

250 "Theological Education in the Anglican Communion," Anglican Communion Office, 2005.

251 Ndungane, *A World With a Human Face,* 76.

252 Statement issued by Anglican Archbishop Njongonkulu Ndungane on the election and Consecration of Gene Robinson as bishop of New Hampshire, November 2003.

253 Ndungane, *A World With a Human Face*, 110.

254 Sharon LaFraniere, "Inviting Africa's Anglicans to Gather Under a Bigger Tent," *The New York Times,* February 10, 2007, A4.

255 Luke Pato, "Anglicanism and Africanisation," *Journal of Theology for Southern Africa* 101 (July 1998), 50.

256 Ndungane, *A World With a Human Face*, 111.

257 "Ndungane takes Government to Task over AIDS," Cape Argus, 1 December 2004.

258 Pato, "Anglicanism and Africanisation," 54.

259 Pato, "Anglicanism and Africanisation," 52. There may still be advantages to the perception of England as home. I remember having a conversation with the Bishop of Gambia, the first Gambian to hold the post. He said he had just returned from "home leave," a perquisite still in the bishop's contract that provided for him and his family to return "home" to England for four months every several years.

260 "A Gay Dialogue," *Journal of Theology for Southern Africa* 121 (March 2005), 71. The resolution cited is Resolution I.10 of the 1998 Lambeth Conference: "This Conference cannot advise the legitimizing or blessing of same sex unions nor ordaining those involved in same gender unions."

261 In Longley's letter of invitation to the first Lambeth Conference, he wrote: "Such a meeting would not be competent to make declarations or lay down definitions on points of doctrine." See Chapter I.

262 Andrew Linzey, "Mistakes of the Creator," in Andrew Linzey, ed., *Gays and the Future of Anglicanism: Responses to the Windsor Report* (Winchester: O Books, 2005), xxxii. The normative mode of governance in Anglicanism has always been synodical, in which concurrence among bishops, clergy and laypeople has been understood as necessary for enacting legislation and setting policy. The usefulness of Lambeth, therefore, especially in a climate that values lay ministry, has been questioned. This is why Archbishop Ndungane advocated for an Anglican gathering involving all orders of ministry in conjunction with the Lambeth Conference originally slated to take place in Cape Town in 2008.

263 James E. Solheim, *Diversity or Disunity: Reflections on Lambeth 1998.* (New York: Church Publishing, 1999, 79. It is noteworthy that there was a greater number of bishops who signed the apology than who voted against the resolution. This is because many felt the resolution was theologically sound but pastorally insensitive.

264 Andrew Linzey, "Mistakes of the Creator," xxxi.

265 John Kater, "Faithful Church, Plural World," 258. At a conference called "Hope and a Future," held in Pittsburgh 10–12 November 2005 and sponsored by the Network of Anglican Communion Dioceses and Parishes, Archbishop Datuk Yong Ping Chung, whose province, Southeast Asia, does not ordain women, said that the question of whether to ordain women "is not a Communion-breaking issue. We ask that those who ordain women respect our position, as we respect theirs."

266 Njongonkulu Ndungane, Report on Section I, "Called to Full Humanity," Theme 3, Human Sexuality, 29 April 1997. Ndungane compared homosexuality with "other forms of behavior which some Christians claim should not be regarded as inherently sinful but which may be less than complete expressions of the Christian way. These would include some forms of African traditional marriage and faithful cohabitation."

267 Solheim, *Diversity or Disunity*, 75.

268 Peter Gomes, *The Good Book: Reading Bible with Mind and Heart.* (New York: Morrow, 1996), 95.

269 Philip Russell, *The Bible and Homosexuality: What is the Spirit saying to the Churches?* (Cape Town: CPSA Publishing Department, 2005), 7, emphasis mine.

270 e.g., Titus 2:9 requiring slaves to be submissive to their masters; Paul's statements about the superiority of men over women, e.g., 1 Cor 11:2, and both Jesus' and Paul's statements on the dissolubility of marriage which make divorce unacceptable for the Christian.

271 Russell, *The Bible and Homosexuality*, 11.

272 Ibid., 13–16.

273 "Being Human – A Christian understanding of personhood illustrated with reference to power, money, sex and time," Report of the Doctrine Committee of the General Synod of the Church of England, Church House London, 2003, 80–81.

274 David Russell, "A Theological Reflection on Human Sexuality," address delivered at Provincial Synod, Pinetown, KwaZulu Natal, July 2005.

275 cited in Solheim, *Diversity or Disunity*, 70–71..

276 John L. Kater, Jr. "Faithful Church, Plural World: Diversity and Lambeth 1998," *Anglican Theological Review,* Vol. 81, No. 2 (1999, 256.

277 Richard Hooker, *Laws of Ecclesiastical Polity* III, cited in John Kater, "Faithful Church, Plural World," 253.

278 Hope and a Future Conference, Pittsburgh, Pennsylvania, 11 November 2005.

279 "No Debate on Gays, says Orombi," *The New Vision*, 4 March 2005.

280 John Kater, "Faithful Church, Plural World," 257.

281 Khotso Makhulu, "People of Encounter," *Anglican World* (Michaelmas 1998) 5.

282 Paul Germond, "Sex in a Globalizing World: The South African Churches and the Crisis of Sexuality," *Journal of Theology for Southern Africa* 119 (July 2004) 50–51.

283 Presiding Bishop Frank Griswold, "Remarks on Windsor Report," 18 October 2004.

284 Kevin Ward, "African Perspectives on Episcopacy and Sexuality," Andrew Linzey and Richard Kirker, eds., *Gays and the Future of*

Anglicanism, 243.

285 Njongonkulu Ndungane, "The key is not sex, but relationships," *This Day* (Johannesburg daily) 3 December 2003.

286 quoted in Stephen Bates, "African cleric breaks ranks on gay issue," *The Guardian,* 8 September 2003.

287 R. William Franklin, "Lambeth 1998," 264.

288 Kater, "Faithful Church, Plural World," 242.

289 cited in Germond, 51.

290 Kater, "Faithful Church, Plural World," 240–241.

291 The comments of E. Don Taylor, vicar bishop of New York and a native of Jamaica about the work of English missionaries among West Indians are applicable as well to the African experience. He observes that small island communities provided a favorable unit for complete indoctrination. English life was "packaged in so skillful a manner that everything worthwhile had to be English or white, everything contrary was just bad." ("Tensions and Opportunities between West Indian and American Blacks," *St. Luke's Journal of Theology* 22, No. 4 (September, 1979), 277.)

292 Kater, "Faithful Church, Plural World," 241.

293 Kevin Ward, "African Perspectives on Episcopacy and Sexuality," in ed. Andrew Linzey, *Gays and the Future of Anglicanism*, 250.

294 Such attitudes are rife in the missionary hymns of Reginald Heber. "From Greenland's icy mountains," for example, contains the words: *In vain with lavish kindness the gifts of God are strown; The heathen in his blindness bows down to wood and stone. Shall we whose souls are lighted with wisdom from on high Shall we to those benighted the lamp of life deny?* (*The Hymnal 1940*, 254)

295 Statement from Archbishop Peter Akinola, Primate of the Church of Nigeria, Anglican Consultative Council, Hong Kong, 25 September 2002.

296 Statement of the Bishops of the Province of the Anglican Church in South East Asia, 13 August 2003.

297 Statement by the Most Rev. Mpalanyi Nkoyoyo, Archbishop of the Church of the Province of Uganda, October 2003, emphasis mine.

298 Willis Jenkins, "Episcopalians, Homosexuality, and World Mission," *Anglican Theology Review*, Vol. 86, No.2 (2004), 298.

299 Kater, "Faithful Church, Plural World," 259.

300 Comments by Bishop Nuttall were made in an interview with the author held in Pietermaritzburg on 28 July 2005.

301 Comments by Archbishop Tutu were made in an interview with the author in Cape Town on 4 August 2004.

302 The other sections were "Called to live and proclaim the Good News," "Called to be a faithful Church in a plural world," and "Called to be one."

303 Book of Common Prayer (ECUSA) 1979, 305.

304 Comments by Professor Draper were made in an interview with the author in Pietermaritzburg, 27 July 2005.

305 "Our need for moral honesty," speech delivered 10 October 2003, Cape Town.

306 Comments by Archbishop Ndungane were made in an interview with the author in Toronto, 21 July 2005.

307 Comments by Bishop Thabo were made in an interview with the author in Grahamstown, 2 August 2004.

308 Janet Trisk, interview with the author in Grahamstown, 5 August 2005.

309 cited in *Seek* (formerly a monthly publication of the CPSA), Cape Town, June 1983.

310 Roy Barker, "Edward Laurie King: An Appreciation," in England and Patterson, *Bounty in Bondage: The Anglican Church in Southern Africa* (Johannesburg: Raven Press, 1989), 6.

311 Ibid., 9.

312 Ibid., 6.

313 The comments by Archbishop Tutu were made during an interview with the author in Cape Town on 4 August 2004.

314 Njongonkulu Ndungane. "Scripture: What Is at Issue in Anglicanism Today?" Ian T. Douglas and Kwok Pui-Lan, eds. *Beyond Colonial Anglicanism: The Anglican Communion in the Twenty-first Century.* New York: Church Publishing, 2001, 235-246. Unless otherwise noted, Ndungane's comments on the relationship between Scripture and homosexuality are gleaned from this article.

315 "Ndungane prays for creative solutions on gays," *Christians for Truth*, Kranskop, South Africa, 17 June 2004.

316 "Our need for moral honesty," *Church Times*, London, 10 October 2003.

317 Sermon preached in Washington National Cathedral, 30 January 2004.

318 Ibid.

319 See, for example, George Sumner, "After Dromantine," *Anglican Theological Review* (Fall 2005) Vol. 87, No. 4, 559ff.

320 In some places where such rites have not been authorized, notably in the USA, various forms of same-sex blessings have been allowed to take place nevertheless.

321 The vote was so narrow, in fact, that had the American and Canadian representatives been allowed to vote, the resolution to accept their voluntary withdrawal would not have passed.

322 *To Set Our Hope in Christ,* The Office of Communication, Episcopal Church Center, New York, 2005.

323 Peter Hinchfliffe, *The Anglican Church in South Africa* (London, 1963), 94–95.

324 BBC interview with Sir David Frost, 12 October 2003.

325 Njongonkulu Ndungane, "Anglicans in Communion: Rhetoric or Reality," Keynote address, Theological Hui, Auckland, NZ, 16 August 2005.

326 Njongonkulu Ndungane, "Journey to Wholeness," the Archbishop's Charge to the 29th Provincial Synod of the CPSA.

327 See esp. Desmond Tutu, *No Future Without Forgiveness* (New York: Doubleday, 1997), chapter 2.

328 See Harold T. Lewis, "Covenant, Contract and Communion: Reflections on a Post-Windsor Anglicanism," *Anglican Theological Review*, Vol. 87, No. 4, (Fall 2005), 601–607.

329 Lorraine Cavanagh, "The Freeing of Anglican Identities," *Theology Wales,* special issue: The Church and Homosexuality: A Contribution to the Debate, Cardiff, 2004.

330 Richard Hooker, *Laws of Ecclesiastical Polity,* I.1.2. (Cambridge, Mass.: Belknap Press of Harvard University, 1977).

331 In my article, I suggest that the difference between "covenant" and "contract" is that the former is predicated upon trust whereas the latter is strictly legal. The covenant, a document to which all provinces of the Communion would be expected to subscribe, as suggested by Dr. Williams is, I believe, closer to my definition of "contract." See Lewis, "Covenant, Contract and Communion: Reflections on a Post-Windsor Anglicanism," *Anglican Theological Review* 87, No. 4, esp. 601–602.

332 Report of the Covenant Design Group, ACNS 4252, 19 February 2007.

333 The Communiqué of the Primates' Meeting in Dar es Salaam, ACNS

4263, 19 February 2007.

334   The Windsor Report's language used the adverb "until." Windsor held open the possibility, however remote, that at some future date, even decades hence, a new understanding about human sexuality might emerge, as has been the case with polygamy, for example. The Tanzanian document seems to negate such an eventuality.

335   "A Communication to the Episcopal Church from the March 2007 Meeting of the House of Bishops," Episcopal News Service, 20 March 2007.

336   Statement on the Windsor Report, 18 October 2004.

337   "The Archbishop of Cape Town responds to the Archbishop of Canterbury," reported in *Daily Episcopalian,* 28 June 2006.

338   Njongonkulu Ndungane, Foreword, in ed. Jonathan A. Draper, *The Eye of the Storm: Bishop John William Colenso and the Crisis of Biblical Interpretation,* Pietermaritzburg, 2003, 1.

339   Sermon preached in Washington National Cathedral, 1 February 2004.

340   John William Colenso, *The Pentateuch and the Book of Joshua Critically Examined,* 1865, I.10.

341   Address delivered at the "Healing Leaves" Conference, Berkeley, California, 20 January 2000, ACNS 2009/2010, 7 February 2000.

342   Book of Common Prayer (The Episcopal Church, 1979), 305.

343   Bruce Kay, *Reinventing Anglicanism: A Vision of Confidence, Community and Engagement in Anglican Christianity* (New York: Church Publishing, 2003), 45.

344   Bishop Philip David Russell, "A Theological Reflection on Human Sexuality," address delivered at the Provincial Synod of the CPSA, July 2005, Pine Town, KwaZulu, Natal.

BIBLIOGRAPHY

Allen, John. *Rabble-Rouser for Peace: The Authorised Biography of Desmond Tutu.* London: Random House, 2006.

Battle, Michael. *Reconciliation: The Ubuntu Theology of Desmond Tutu.* Cleveland: The Pilgrim Press, 1997.

———, ed. *The Wisdom of Tutu.* Louisville: Knox Westminster Press, 1988.

Brilioth, Yngve. *The Anglican Revival: Studies in the Oxford Movement.* London: Longmans, Green, 1933.

Charry, Ellen T. "Christian Witness to Contemporary Culture Regarding Sex," *Anglican Theological Review*, Vol. 86, No. 2, 2004, 273–292.

Clarke, C.P.S. *The Oxford Movement and After.* London: Mowbray, 1932.

Denniston, Robin. *Trevor Huddleston: A Life.* New York: St. Martin's Press, 1999.

De Gruchy, John W. *The Church Struggle in South Africa.* Grand Rapids: Eerdmans, 1979.

———. *Theology and Ministry in Context and Crisis: A South African Perspective.* Grand Rapids: Eerdmans, 1986.

Douglas, Ian T. and Kwok Pui-Lan, eds. *Beyond Colonial Anglicanism: The Anglican Communion in the Twenty-first Century.* New York: Church Publishing, 2001.

————. "Inculturation and Anglican Worship," ed. Charles Hefling and Cynthia Shattuck. *The Oxford Guide to the Book of Common Prayer: A Worldwide Survey.* New York: Oxford University Press, 2006, 273ff.

Draper, Jonathan A. "Bishop John William Colenso and History as Unfolding Narrative," *Journal of Theology for Southern Africa*, 117, November, 2003, 97ff.

————, ed. *Commentary on the Romans by John William Colenso.* Pietermaritzburg: Cluster Publications, 2003.

————, ed. *The Eye of the Storm: Bishop John William Colenso and the Crisis of Biblical Interpretation.* Pietermaritzburg: Cluster Publications, 2003.

————. "A 'Frontier' Reading of Romans: The Case of Bishop John William Colenso (1814-1883)," ed.. Yeo khiok-khing, *Navigating Romans through Cultures,* 1ff. London: Clark, Ltd., 2004.

Du Boulay, Shirley. *Tutu: Voice of the Voiceless.* London: Penguin Books, 1988.

England, Frank and Torquil Paterson eds. *Bounty in Bondage: The Anglican Church in Southern Africa.* Johannesburg: Raven Press, 1989.

Faber, Geoffrey. *Oxford Apostles: A Character Study of the Oxford Movement.* London: Faber & Faber, 1933.

Germond, Paul. "Sex in a Globalizing World: The South African Churches and the Crisis of Sexuality," *Journal of Theology for Southern Africa* 119 (July 2004) 46–58.

Giljam, Miles, "Desmond Tutu: Toward Freedom and Justice," *Southern Anglican,* Vol. 1, June 2004, 20–23.

Gomes, Peter J. *The Good Book: Reading the Bible With Mind and Heart.* New York: Morrow, 1996, (chapter 6 "The Bible and Homosexuality").

Guma, Mongezi and Leslie Milton, eds. *An African Challenge to the Church in the 21st Century.* Cape Town: The Methodist Church of Southern Africa, 1997.

Guy, Jeff. *The Heretic: A Study of the Life of John William Colenso 1814–1883.* Johannesburg: Raven Press, 1983.

Hefling, Charles, ed. *Our Selves, our Souls and Bodies: Sexuality and the Household of God.* Boston: Cowley Publications, 1996.

Hinchcliff, Peter. *The Anglican Church in South Africa: An account of the history and development of the Church in the Province of South Africa.* London: Darton, 1963.

———. *John William Colenso, Bishop of Natal.* London: Nelson, 1964.

Honore, Deborah Duncan, ed. *Trevor Huddleston: Essays in his Life and Work.* Oxford: The University Press, 1988.

Huddleston, Trevor, C.R. *Naught for Your Comfort.* Garden City, NY: Doubleday, 1956.

Hylson-Smith, Kenneth. *High Churchmanship in the Church of England—From the Sixteenth Century to the Late Twentieth Century.* Edinburgh: T&T Clark, 1993.

Jardine, Alexander Johnstone. *A Fragment of Church History at the Cape of Good Hope.* Originally published by Bridekirk, Heerghracht, 1827. South African Library Reprint Series, 1979.

Jenkins, Willis. "Episcopalians, Homosexuality and World Mission," *Anglican Theological Review,* Vol. 86, No. 2, 2004, 293–316.

———. "Ethnohomophia?" *Anglican Theological Review,* Vol. 82, No. 3, 2000.

Kaye, Bruce. *Reinventing Anglicanism: A Vision of Confidence, community and engagement in Anglican Christianity.* New York: Church Publishing, 2005.

Lafraniere, Sharon. "Inviting Africa's Anglicans to Gather Under a Bigger Tent," (interview with Archbishop Ndungane) *The New York Times,* February 10, 2007, A4.

Lee, Peter (Bishop of Christ the King). *Compromise and Courage—Anglicans in Johannesburg 1864–1999: A divided church in search of integrity.* Pietermaritzburg: Cluster Publications, 2005.

Lewis, Cecil and G. E. Edwards. *Historical Records of the Church in the Province of South Africa.* London: SPCK, 1934.

Lewis, Harold T. *Christian Social Witness.* Cambridge, Mass.: Cowley Publications, 2001.

———. "Covenant, Contract and Communion," *Anglican Theological Review,* Vol. 87, No.4, (Fall 2005) 601–607.

———. "They called them to deliver their lands from error's chain," *Anglican Theological Review,* Vol. 78, Fall, 1996.

———. *Yet With a Steady Beat: The African American Struggle for Recognition in the Episcopal Church.* Valley Forge, PA: Trinity Press International, 1996.

Lindhorst, Alan, ed. *The Golden Mitre: A Tribute to the life and ministry of Archbishop Robert Selby Taylor.* Cape Town, 1955.

Linzey, Andrew and Richard Kirker, eds. *Gays and the Future of Anglicanism: Reponses to the Windsor Report.* Winchester, UK: O Books, 2005.

Makgoba, Thabo Cecil, "A Vision of Faithful Witness," the Bishop's charge on the occasion of his Enthronement as bishop of Grahamstown, Cathedral Church of SS. Michael & George, 14 February 2004.

Mayson, Cedric. *A Certain Sound: The Struggle for Liberation in South Africa.* Maryknoll, NY: Orbis Books, 1984.

May, J. Lewis. *The Oxford Movement.* London: John Lane, 1933.

Ndungane, Njongonkulu. "An Optimistic View of our Anglican Future," *Southern Anglican,* Vol. 11, December 2006, 10–16.

Ndungane, Njongonkulu. "The Church's Struggle: The Church's Role in South African Liberation," *Southern Anglican,* Vol. 1, June 2004, 10–18.

———. "The Key is not sex, but relationships," *This Day,* (Johannesburg daily) December 3, 2003.

———. *A World with a Human Face: A Voice from Africa.* Cape Town: David Philip, 2003.

Nicolson, Ronald. "A Gay Dialogue," *Journal of Theology for Southern Africa* 121 (March 2005) 71–87.

Nuttall, Michael. *Number Two to Tutu: A Memoir.* Pietermaritzburg: Cluster Publications, 2003.

———. "The Province of Southern Africa," ed. Charles Hefling and Cynthia Shattuck. *The Oxford Guide to the Book of Common Prayer: A Worldwide Survey.* New York: Oxford University Press, 2006, 315ff.

Page, B. T. *The Harvest of Good Hope: An account of the expansion of the Church of the Province of South Africa.* London: SPCK, 1947.

Pato, Luke Lungile. "Anglicanism and Africanisation: The Legacy of Robert Gray," *Journal of Theology for Southern Africa,* Vol. 101 (July 1998) 49–57.

Paton, Alan. *Apartheid and the Archbishop: The Life and Times of Geoffrey Clayton, Archbishop of Cape Town.* Cape Town: David Philip, 1973.

Peart-Binns, John S. *Archbishop Joost deBlank, Scourge of Apartheid.* London: Miller, Blond & White, 1987.

Russell, Bishop David. *The Bible and Homosexuality: What is the Spirit saying to the Churches?* Cape Town: CPSA Publishing Department, 2004.

Simpson, James B. and Edward M. Story. *The Long Shadows of Lambeth X.* New York: McGraw Hill, 1969.

Solheim, James E. *Diversity or Unity? Reflections on Lambeth 1998.* New York: Church Publishing, 1999.

Stephenson, Alan M.G. *Anglicanism and the Lambeth Conferences.* London: SPCK, 1978.

———. *The First Lambeth Conference 1867.* London: SPCK, 1967.

Tlhagale, Buti and Itumeleng Mosala. *Hammering Swords Into Ploughshares: Essays in Honor of Archbishop Mpilo Desmond Tutu.* Grand Rapids: Eerdmans, 1986.

Tutu, Desmond. *Crying in the Wilderness: The Struggle for Justice in South Africa.* London: Mowbray, 1982.

———. "Dark Days: Episcopal Ministry in Times of Repression, 1976–1996," *Journal of Theology for Southern Africa* 118 (March 2004) 27–39.

———. *Hope and Suffering. Sermons and Speeches.* London: Collins, 1983.

————. Lecture, delivered at the inaugural "Naught for Your Comfort" Lecture, Church of Christ the King, Sophiatown, 7 August 2004.

————. *No Future Without Forgiveness*. New York: Doubleday, 1997.

Worsnip, Michael E. *Between Two Fires: The Anglican Church and Apartheid 1948 to 1957*. Pietermaritzburg: University of Natal Press, 1991.